HIGH SCHOOL
TALKSHEETS

Psalms and Proverbs—Updated!

50
DISCUSSION STARTERS
FOR HIGH SCHOOL YOUTH GROUPS

RICK BUNDSCHUH & TOM FINLEY

ZONDERVAN

Youth Specialties
.com

ZONDERVAN.com/
AUTHORTRACKER
follow your favorite authors

ZONDERVAN

High School TalkSheets Psalms and Proverbs—Updated! 50 discussion starters for high school youth groups
Copyright © 2001 by Youth Specialties

Youth Specialties products, 300 S. Pierce St., El Cajon, CA 92020, are published by Zondervan, 5300 Patterson Ave. S.E., Grand Rapids, MI 49530

Library of Congress Cataloging-in-Publication Data

Bundschuh, Rick, 1951-
    High school talksheets from Psalms & Proverbs, updated! : 50 creative discussion starters from the Old Testament / Rick Bundschuh and Tom Finley.
        p. cm.
    ISBN-13: 978-0-310-23853-9
    1. Bible. O.T. Psalms—Study and teaching. 2. Bible. O.T. Proverbs—Study and teaching. 3. High School students—Religious life. 4. Church group work with teenagers. I. Title: High school talk sheets from Psalms and Proverbs, updated. II. Finley, Tom, 1951- III. Title.

BS1451 .B85 2001
223'.2'00712—dc21
                                                                              00-043934

Web site addresses listed in this book were current at the time of publication, but we can't guarantee they're still operational. If you have trouble with a URL, please contact us via email (YS@YouthSpecialties.com) to let us know if you've found the correct or new URL or if the URL is no longer operational.

Edited by Mary Fletcher, Anita Palmer, and Tamara Rice
Cover and interior design by PAZ Design Group
Illustrations and borders by Rick Sealock

Printed in the United States of America

CONTENTS

HIGH SCHOOL TalkSheets

Psalms and Proverbs—Updated!

CONTENTS

THE HOWS AND WHATS OF TALKSHEETS

You are holding a very valuable book! No, it won't make you a genius or millionaire. But it does contain 50 instant discussions for high school kids. Inside you'll find reproducible TalkSheets that cover a variety of hot topics—plus simple, step-by-step instructions on how to use them. All you need is this book, a few copies of the handouts, and some kids (and maybe a snack or two). You're on your way to landing on some serious issues in kids' lives today.

These TalkSheets are user-friendly and very flexible. They can be used in a youth group meeting, a Sunday school class, or in a Bible study group. You can adapt them for either large or small groups. And they can be covered in only 20 minutes or explored more intensively in two hours.

You can build an entire youth group meeting around a single TalkSheet, or you can use TalkSheets to supplement other materials and resources you might be using. These are tools for you—how you use them is your choice.

High School TalkSheets Psalms and Proverbs—Updated! is not your average curriculum or workbook. This collection of discussions will get your kids involved and excited about talking through important issues. The TalkSheets deal with key topics and include interesting activities, challenging questions, and eye-catching graphics. They will challenge your kids to think about opinions, learn about themselves, and grow in their faith.

LEADING A TALKSHEET DISCUSSION

TalkSheets can be used as a curriculum for your youth group, but they are designed to be springboards for discussion. They encourage your kids to take part and interact with each other while talking about real life issues. And hopefully they'll do some serious thinking,

discover new ideas for themselves, defend their points of view, and make decisions.

Youth today face a world of moral confusion. Teenagers are bombarded with the voices of society and media messages—most of which drown out what they hear from the church. Youth leaders must teach the church's beliefs and values—and also help young people make the right choices in a world with so many options.

A TalkSheet discussion works for this very reason. While dealing with the questions and activities on the TalkSheet, your kids will think carefully about issues, compare their beliefs and values with others, and make their own choices. TalkSheets will challenge your group to explain and rework their ideas in a Christian atmosphere of acceptance, support, and growth.

The most common fear of high school youth group leaders is, "What will I do if the kids in my group just sit there and don't say anything?" Well, when kids don't have anything to say, it's because they haven't had a chance or time to get their thoughts organized! Most young people haven't developed the ability to think on their feet. Since many are afraid they might sound stupid, they don't know how to voice their ideas and opinions.

The solution? TalkSheets let your kids deal with the issues in a challenging, non-threatening way before the actual discussion begins. They'll have time to organize their thoughts, write them down, and ease their fears about participating. They may even look forward to sharing their answers! Most importantly, they'll (most likely) want to find out what others said and open up to talk through the topics.

If you're still a little leery about the success of a real discussion among your kids, that's okay! The only way to get them rolling is to get them started.

YOUR ROLE AS THE LEADER

The best discussions don't happen by accident. They require careful preparation and a sensitive leader. Don't worry if you aren't experienced or don't have hours to prepare.

TalkSheets are designed to help even the novice leader! The more TalkSheet discussions you lead, the easier it becomes. Keep the following tips in mind when using the TalkSheets as you get your kids talking.

BE CHOOSY

Each TalkSheet deals with a different topic. Choose a TalkSheet based on the needs and the maturity level of your group. Don't feel obligated to use the TalkSheets in the order they appear in this book. Use your best judgment and mix them up however you want—they are tools for you!

MAKE COPIES

Kids will need their own copies of the TalkSheet. Only make copies of the student's side of the TalkSheet! The material on the reverse side (the leader's guide) is just for you. You're able to make copies for your group because we've given you permission to do so. U.S. copyright laws have not changed, and it is still mandatory to request permission from a publisher before making copies of other published material. It is against the law not to do so. However, permission is given for you to make copies of this material for your group only, not for every youth group in your state. Thank you for cooperating.

TRY IT YOURSELF

Once you have chosen a TalkSheet for your group, answer the questions and do the activities yourself. Imagine your kids' reactions to the TalkSheet. This will help you prepare for the discussion and understand what you are asking them to do. Plus, you'll have some time to think of other appropriate questions, activities, and Bible verses.

GET SOME INSIGHT

On each leader's guide page, you'll find numerous tips and ideas for getting the most out of your discussion. You may want to add some of your own thoughts or ideas in the margins. And there's room to keep track of the date and the name of your group at the top of the leader's page. You'll also find suggestions for additional activities and discussion questions.

There are some references to Internet links throughout the TalkSheets. These are guides for you to find the resources and information that you need. For additional help, be sure to visit the Youth Specialties Web site at www.YouthSpecialties.com for information on materials and further links to finding what you need.

INTRODUCE THE TOPIC

It's important to introduce the topic before you pass out the TalkSheets to your group. Depending on your group, keep it short and to the point. Be careful not to over-introduce the topic, sound preachy, or resolve the issue before you've started. Your goal is to spark their interest and leave plenty of room for discussion.

The best way to do this is verbally. You can tell a story, share an experience, or describe a situation or problem having to do with the topic. You might want to jump-start your group by asking something like, "What is the first thing you think of when you hear the word _____ [insert the topic]?" Then, after a few answers have been given, you can add something like, "Well, it seems we all have different ideas about this subject. Tonight we're going to investigate it a bit further..." Then pass out the TalkSheet and be sure that everyone has a pencil or pen. Now you're on your way! The following are excellent methods you can use to introduce any topic in this book—

- Show a related short film or video.
- Read a passage from a book or magazine that relates to the subject.
- Play a popular CD that deals with the topic.
- Perform a short skit or dramatic presentation.
- Play a simulation game or role-play, setting up the topic.
- Present current statistics, survey results, or read a current newspaper article that provides recent information about the topic.
- Use an icebreaker or other crowd game, getting into the topic in a humorous way. For example if the topic is fun, play a game to begin the discussion. If the topic is success, consider a

game that helps the kids experience success or failure.

- Use posters, videos, or any other visuals to help focus attention on the topic.

There are endless possibilities for an intro—you are limited only by your own creativity! Each TalkSheet offers a few suggestions, but you are free to use any method with which you feel comfortable. But do keep in mind that the introduction is a very important part of each session.

SET BOUNDARIES

It'll be helpful to set a few ground rules before the discussion. Keep the rules to a minimum, of course, but let the kids know what's expected of them. Here are suggestions for some basic ground rules—

- **What is said in this room stays in this room.** Emphasize the importance of confidentiality. Confidentiality is vital for a good discussion. If your kids can't keep the discussion in the room, then they won't open up.
- **No put-downs.** Mutual respect is important. If your kids disagree with some opinions, ask them to comment on the subject (but not on the other person). It's okay to attack the ideas, but not other people.
- **There is no such thing as a dumb question.** Your group members must feel free to ask questions at any time. The best way to learn is to ask questions and get answers.
- **No one is forced to talk.** Some kids will open up, some won't. Let everyone know they have the right to pass or not answer any question.
- **Only one person speaks at a time.** This is a mutual respect issue. Everyone's opinion is worthwhile and deserves to be heard.

Communicate with your group that everyone needs to respect these boundaries. If you sense that your group members are attacking each other or getting a negative attitude during the discussion, do stop and deal with the problem before going on.

ALLOW ENOUGH TIME

Pass out copies of the TalkSheet to your kids after the introduction and make sure that each person has a pen or pencil and a Bible. There are usually five or six activities on each TalkSheet. If your time

is limited, or if you are using only a part of the TalkSheet, tell the group to complete only the activities you'd like them to.

Decide ahead of time whether or not you would like the kids to work on the TalkSheets individually or in groups.

Let them know how much time they have for completing the TalkSheet and let them know when there is a minute (or so) left. Go ahead and give them some extra time and then start the discussion when everyone seems ready to go.

SET THE STAGE

Create a climate of acceptance. Most teenagers are afraid to voice their opinions because they don't want to be laughed at or look stupid in front of their peers. They want to feel safe if they're going to share their feelings and beliefs. Communicate that they can share their thoughts and ideas—even if they may be different or unpopular. If your kids get put-downs, criticism, laughter, or snide comments (even if their statements are opposed to the teachings of the Bible) it'll hurt the discussion.

Always phrase your questions—even those that are printed on the TalkSheets—so that you are asking for an opinion, not an answer. For example if a question reads, "What should Bill have done in that situation?" change it to, "What do you think Bill should have done in that situation?" The simple addition of the three words "do you think" makes the question less threatening and a matter of opinion, rather than a demand for the right answer. Your kids will relax when they will feel more comfortable and confident. Plus, they'll know that you actually care about their opinions and they'll feel appreciated!

LEAD THE DISCUSSION

Discuss the TalkSheet with the group and encourage all your kids to participate. Communicate that it's important for them to respect each other's opinions and feelings! The more they contribute, the better the discussion will be.

If your youth group is big, you may divide it into smaller groups of six to 12. Each of these small groups should have a facilitator—either an adult leader or a student member—to keep the discussion going. Remind the facilitators not to dominate. If the group looks to the facilitator for an answer, ask him or her to direct the question or responses back to the group. Once the smaller groups have completed their discussions, combine them into one large group and ask the different groups to share their ideas.

You don't have to divide the groups up with every TalkSheet. For some discussions, you may want to vary the group size or to divide the meeting into groups of the same sex.

The discussion should target the questions and answers on the TalkSheet. Go through them one at a time and ask the kids to share their responses. Have them compare their answers and brainstorm new ones in addition to the ones they've written down. Encourage them to share their opinions and answers, but don't force those who are quiet.

AFFIRM ALL RESPONSES—RIGHT OR WRONG

Let your kids know that their comments and contributions are appreciated and important. This is especially true for those who rarely speak up in group activities. Make a point of thanking them for joining in. This will be an incentive for them to participate further.

Remember that affirmation doesn't mean approval. Affirm even those comments that seem wrong to you. You'll show that everyone has a right to express ideas—no matter how controversial those ideas may be. If someone states an opinion that is off base, make a mental note of the comment. Then in your wrap-up, come back to the comment or present a different point of view in a positive way. But don't reprimand the student who voiced the comment.

DON'T BE THE AUTHORITATIVE ANSWER

Some kids think you have the right answer to every question. They'll look to you for approval, even when they are answering another group member's question. If they start to focus on you for answers, redirect them toward the group by making a comment like, "Remember that you're talking to everyone, not just me."

Your goal as the facilitator is to keep the discussion alive and kicking. It's important that your kids think of you as a member of the group—on their level. The less authoritative you are, the more value your own opinions will have. If your

kids view you as a peer, they will listen to your comments. You have a tremendous responsibility to be, with sincerity, their trusted friend.

LISTEN TO EACH PERSON

God gave you one mouth and two ears. Good discussion leaders know how to listen. Although it's tempting at times, don't monopolize the discussion. Encourage others to talk first—then express your opinions during your wrap up.

DON'T FORCE IT

Encourage all your kids to talk, but don't make them comment. Each member has the right to pass. If you feel that the discussion isn't going well, go on to the next question or restate the question to keep them moving.

DON'T TAKE SIDES

You'll probably have different opinions expressed in the group from time to time. Be extra careful not to take one side or another. Encourage both sides to think through their positions—ask questions to get them deeper. If everyone agrees on an issue, you can play devil's advocate with tough questions and stretch their thinking. Remain neutral—your point of view is your own, not that of the group.

DON'T LET ANYONE (INCLUDING YOU) TAKE OVER

Nearly every youth group has one person who likes to talk and is perfectly willing to express an opinion on any subject. Try to encourage equal participation from all the kids.

SET UP FOR THE TALK

Make sure that the seating arrangement is inclusive and encourages a comfortable, safe atmosphere for discussion. Theater-style seating (in rows) isn't discussion-friendly. Instead, arrange the chairs in a circle or semicircle (or on the floor with pillows!).

LET THEM LAUGH!

Discussions can be fun! Most of the TalkSheets include questions that'll make kids laugh and get them thinking, too.

LET THEM BE SILENT

Silence can be scary for discussion leaders! Some react by trying to fill the silence with a question or a comment. The following suggestions may help you to handle silence more effectively—

- Be comfortable with silence. Wait it out for 30 seconds or so to respond. You may want to restate the question to give your kids a gentle nudge.
- Talk about the silence with the group. What does the silence mean? Do they really not have any comments? Maybe they're confused, embarrassed, or don't want to share.
- Answer the silence with questions or comments like, "I know this is challenging to think about..." or "It's scary to be the first to talk." If you acknowledge the silence, it may break the ice.
- Ask a different question that may be easier to handle or that will clarify the one already posed. But don't do this too quickly without giving them time to think the first one through.

KEEP IT UNDER CONTROL

Monitor the discussion. Be aware if the discussion is going in a certain direction or off track. This can happen fast, especially if the kids disagree or things get heated. Mediate wisely and set the tone that you want. If your group gets bored with an issue, get them back on track. Let the discussion unfold, but be sensitive to your group and who is or is not getting involved.

If a student brings up a side issue that's interesting, decide whether or not to pursue it. If discussion is going well and the issue is worth discussion, let them talk it through. But, if things get way off track, say something like, "Let's come back to that subject later if we have time. Right now, let's finish our discussion on..."

BE CREATIVE AND FLEXIBLE

You don't have to follow the order of the questions on the TalkSheet. Follow your own creative instinct. If you find other ways to use the TalkSheets, use them! Go ahead and add other questions or Bible references.

Don't feel pressured to spend time on every single activity. If you're short on time, you can skip some items. Stick with the questions that are the most interesting to the group.

SET YOUR GOALS

TalkSheets are designed to move along toward a goal, but you need to identify your goal in advance. What would you like your young people to learn? What truth should they discover? What is the goal of the session? If you don't know where you're going, it's doubtful you will get there.

BE THERE FOR YOUR KIDS

Some kids may want to talk more with you (you got 'em thinking!). Let them know that you can talk one-on-one with them afterwards.

Communicate to the kids that they can feel free to talk with you about anything with confidentiality. Let them know you're there for them with support and concern, even after the TalkSheet discussion has been completed.

USE THE BIBLE

Most adults believe the Bible has authority over their lives. It's common for adults to start their discussions or to support their arguments with Bible verses. But today's teenagers form their opinions and beliefs from their own life situations first—then they decide how the Bible fits their needs. TalkSheets start with the realities of the adolescent world and then move toward the Bible. You'll be able to show them that the Bible can be their guide and that God does have something to say to them about their own unique situations.

The last activity on each TalkSheet uses Bible verses that were chosen for their application to each issue. But they aren't exhaustive. Feel free to add whatever other verses you think would fit well and add to the discussion.

After your kids read the verses, ask them to think how the verses apply to their lives. Summarize the meanings for them.

For example, after reading the passages for "Window to the Soul," you could summarize by saying something like, "God's standards of beauty for a person's inner self are much different than the world's. How can these verses apply to your inner self?"

CLOSE THE DISCUSSION

Present a challenge to the group by asking yourself, "What do I want the kids to remember most from this discussion?" There's your wrap-up! It's important to conclude by affirming the group and offering a summary that ties the discussion together.

Sometimes you won't need a wrap-up. You may want to leave the issue hanging and discuss it in another meeting. That way, your group can think about it more and you can nail down the final ideas later.

TAKE IT FURTHER

On the leader's guide page, you'll find additional discussion activities—labeled More—for following up on the discussion. These aren't a must, but highly recommended. They let the kids reflect upon, evaluate, review, and assimilate what they've learned. These activities may lead to more discussion and better learning.

After you've done the activity, be sure to debrief your kids on the activity, either now or at the next group meeting. A few good questions to ask about the activity are—

- What happened when you did this activity or discussion?

- Was it helpful or a waste of time?

- How did you feel when doing the activity or discussion?

- Did the activity/discussion make you think differently or affect you in any way?

- In one sentence state what you learned from this activity or discussion.

A FINAL WORD TO THE WISE — THAT'S YOU!

Some of these TalkSheets deal with topics that may be sensitive or controversial for your kids. Issues like sexuality or materialism aren't discussed openly in some churches. You're encouraging discussion and inviting your kids to express their opinions. As a result, you may be criticized by parents or others in your church who may not see the importance of such discussions. Use your best judgment. If you suspect that a particular TalkSheet will cause problems, you may not want to use it. Or you may want to tweak a particular TalkSheet and cover only some of the questions. Either way, the potential bad could outweigh the good—better safe than sorry. To avoid any misunderstanding, you may want to give the parents or senior pastor (or whoever else you are accountable to) copies of the TalkSheet before you use it. Let them know the discussion you would like to have and the goal you are hoping to accomplish. Challenge your kids to take their TalkSheet home to talk about it with their parents. How would their parents, as young people, have answered the questions? Your kids may find that their parents understand them better than they thought! Also, encourage them to think of other Bible verses or ways that the TalkSheet applies to their lives.

GOD'S GUIDE TO GODLINESS

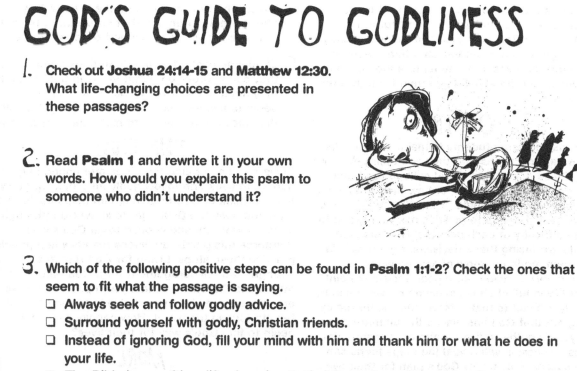

1. Check out **Joshua 24:14-15** and **Matthew 12:30**. What life-changing choices are presented in these passages?

2. Read **Psalm 1** and rewrite it in your own words. How would you explain this psalm to someone who didn't understand it?

3. Which of the following positive steps can be found in **Psalm 1:1-2**? Check the ones that seem to fit what the passage is saying.
   - ❑ Always seek and follow godly advice.
   - ❑ Surround yourself with godly, Christian friends.
   - ❑ Instead of ignoring God, fill your mind with him and thank him for what he does in your life.
   - ❑ The Bible has exciting, life-changing truths! Get to know it and obey it.
   - ❑ People who ridicule God don't really know what he's like. Get to know him!
   - ❑ To be really blessed, choose God's way.

4. Take a look at the following situations, where important choices must be made. Describe which of the steps in question 3 apply to each situation. What you would say to the person in need of help?
   - Alexia never seems to have an opinion of her own. She always goes along what other people say. If she's with wise people, she thinks clearly—if she's in bad company, she stumbles.
   - Chad likes to party and drink with his friends. He knows that it could eventually cause him problems, but he doesn't know how to change.
   - Keanu was in a car crash in which one friend was killed and another was seriously injured. He believes in God but is angry at him—and even feels like rejecting God.
   - Tricia dresses way too provocatively—so much so that even some of the guys think she's weird.
   - Casey is angry because her parents don't trust her. Now she's wondering if it pays to obey their rules.

5. How well are you doing in choosing to go God's way in life? Rate yourself by placing an X on the graph below.

◆ ▮▮▮▮▮▮▮▮▮▮▮▮▮▮▮▮▮▮▮▮ ◆

I'm going only my way.   I'm going all God's way.

GOD'S GUIDE TO GODLINESS [pursuing godliness—Psalm 1]

THIS WEEK

Psalm 1 deals with life's most important issue—choosing to live as God wants his children to. Godly living is often overlooked in today's society, even though it's an essential Christian teaching. This TalkSheet gives your students a look at what godliness is and how they can strive for it in their own lives.

OPENER

Start by asking your students to make a master list of some hard decisions that they and their peers are facing. These may include what college to attend, whether or not to use drugs, or how they'll handle a dating situation. On a scale of 1 to 10 (1 being "This is a very easy decision to make"), ask your group to rank the difficulty of each decision. How many of your kids are facing these decisions right now? Has any of them made (or know of anyone who has made) a smart decision—or a poor decision? Point out that life is full of choices—some of which can be extremely difficult to make. Move into the lesson by pointing out that God has placed the ultimate choice in everyone's path—to live for him or to ignore him. And this discussion will reveal the steps teens can take to successfully follow God's plan for their lives.

THE DISCUSSION, BY NUMBERS

1. These two passages center on choosing to follow God's way rather than some false or useless way. Ask a few of your students to explain what the passages are about—then ask if choosing to live for God is an easy or hard thing to do. How realistic is it to live for God day in and day out? What is the hardest part about doing that?

2. Be sure your kids understand that the psalm warns against lending an open ear to tempting words or sinful advice, following others into sin, and mocking (ridiculing or ignoring) God. Point out that there's wisdom in relying on God's wisdom, which is found in the Bible.

3. Explain that positive steps are steps that people can take to follow God and be blessed (leading happy, meaningful lives). To help explain the third and fifth steps, point out that thanking God can help them think of him often, while prayer and trust will help them get to know him. Is there one step in particular that is less important than the others? What do your students think?

4. These situations give your students a chance to think ahead about ways to deal with similar situations they may face in their lives. What other situations are they facing like these? Talk about practical advice that your students could realistically use in there and other scenarios.

5. Challenge each of your kids to think about what they can improve on. What areas in their lives do they need to give over to God? How can they begin to live for God today? What struggles will they face if they decide to make these changes?

THE CLOSE

Close by summarizing the steps mentioned in question 3—to seek and follow godly advice, keep godly friends, think of God (thanking him helps us do this), read and obey the Bible, get to know God (through prayer and trust), and choose to go God's way. Reinforce this point—godliness results when people practice these steps. Living for God requires strength and encouragement from God—and from others like Christian friends, youth pastors, and others. It's easy to give up and give in to the lies and temptations in the world. How can your students begin to find God's way for their lives?

MORE

● The Christian life is a journey—with ups and downs. How have your students' journeys with God been so far? What ups and downs have they encountered? You may want to have each of your kids describe their own walk with God by mapping out their journeys—showing when the journey started and what ups and downs they've faced since then. How have they handled the struggles and temptations? How have their experiences brought them to where they are today?

● Give your kids some time to examine how well they are doing in the six steps listed in question 3. Challenge them to think of one area they're determined to improve this week and from now on. You may want to sharing one area in your life that you will work on—and ask if any of them want to share theirs too. Be sure to follow up with them later and encourage them to rely on God for strength, patience, and forgiveness.

FINDING HIS PEACE

1. Read the statements and decide if each one is **T (true)** or **F (false)**.
___ The Bible promises that Christians won't ever have troubles.
___ Teenagers struggle more in their faith than adults do.
___ The Bible claims that Christians won't find peace from problems until they go to heaven.
___ Any Christian struggling is a weak Christian.
___ Some Christians never have worries because they can sit back and watch God solve everything.
___ All believers—even the strongest—must learn to trust God in times of trouble.

2. Check out **John 16:33**. What does Jesus say about Christians and problems? What does he say about peace?

3. Now read **Psalm 3** and take a look at the situations below. What promises from Psalm 3 could apply to each situation below?
   - Juan has prepared and worked hard to take a college entrance exam—and he's stressed out. What could most encourage Juan as he studies and faces his worry?

   - Tina is having a hard time finding a summer job, which she really needs to help her family make ends meet. Everywhere she has applied either doesn't have jobs avail able or won't hire her because she's under 18. How could the fact that God sustains Tina help her in this situation?

   - Gina and Scott have vowed to abstain from sex until marriage—but when they're together it's hard to avoid the temptations. Their friends have teased them about it and they both feel the pressure to give in. How can God help Gina and Scott avoid the temptation?

   - Heather's parents have been fighting for months and the family has been under a lot of strain since her dad threatened to move out. What hope and peace can Heather find from God based on Psalm 3?

4. Look up and read the following Bible verses. How do these verses apply to your life?
   Matthew 6:25-26   Philippians 4:6-7   Colossians 3:15   John 14:27

5. Think of a situation that you're facing in your life right now. Are you willing to trust God and let him take care of you? Pick one of the verses above to rewrite in your own words and apply it to your life right now.

FINDING HIS PEACE [God's peace—Psalm 3]

THIS WEEK

There's no doubt that high schoolers face incredible pressure today—rapid physical changes, stress, peer pressure, temptation, and more—how can anyone come through all that in one piece? No matter what, God can get teenagers through it all, serving as their protector and deliverer just as he did to King David so long ago. This TalkSheet will challenge your kids to place their confidence in God and find his peace.

OPENER

How stressed out are your students? You may want to illustrate the effects of stress using one of the suggestions (or one like it) below—

- Place a walnut in a metal nutcracker. As you read your own list of sources of stress, tighten the nutcracker a little. Do this until the nut is crushed.
- How much pressure can an egg take? Hold a raw egg in your hand (or have a volunteer do it!) and squeeze the egg harder when each stressor is read.
- Have a volunteer come to the front of the room, and ask more volunteers to represent each of the stresses on the whiteboard. Every time you read an item from the list, the students representing each stress stand to the side of the volunteer and put their arms tightly around him or her. Do this for eight or more of the stresses mentioned, until the volunteer is so tightly bound that he or she can hardly move. (Just make sure he or she can breathe!)

When you've finished with the list and demonstration, explain that life is full of pressures and stresses. And too much pressure causes people to crack, to get sick physically, or to simply give up.

THE DISCUSSION, BY NUMBERS

1. What do your students think of these statements? Let them debate these among themselves. How true are these statements in their own lives and the lives of their peers?

2. Jesus said that all Christians will have problems on earth—but there's peace for those who take refuge in him. Point out that having his peace doesn't mean that people won't have problems, but instead that God will stand with them and help them work through their problems. How much peace do your kids think God can give them?

3. You may want to summarize the story of Absalom (2 Samuel 15-18), David's son who rebelled against him and caused him to write Psalm 3. Like David, your kids can be sure that God is someone they can turn to even in the worst times. You may want to break your group into smaller discussion clusters for this item.

4. What is your students' peace quotient? Which verses speak to your students? You may want to ask for some to share their thoughts about peace in their lives. Remind them that peace isn't an absence of problems—it's a heartfelt knowledge that God is walking with them through their struggles.

5. How did your kids apply these verses to their lives? You may want to ask for some to share how they re-wrote the verses. How has this TalkSheet helped them understand God's peace in their lives better? What can they do to experience God's peace in their lives today?

THE CLOSE

It's tempting to run from God when trials come—some people don't trust that God is with them and is actually in control of all situations. They want to do things their own way and deal with problems themselves. But who could better help them and give them peace? Challenge your kids to ask God for his peace and direction. When they feel they can't go on with the pressure and stress, he can keep them strong. What changes do you want to make in order to let God give you his peace?

Some kids in your group may be dealing with some critical issues—anything from family divorce to pregnancy. You may want to make yourself available to those who want more personal advice and prayer. Finally, take some time to pray with your group, asking God to help them rely on him with the pressures in their lives.

MORE

- God talks frequently throughout the Bible about trusting in him for his peace. You may want to have your kids look for other verses that talk about resting in him. There are several verses in the Psalms and throughout the Bible. A few include John 14:27, John 16:33, Romans 5:1, Philippians 4:7, and Philippians 4:9. How do these verses compare to David's feelings in Psalm 3?
- The media deals with teen pressures in different ways. A lot of high schoolers learn to deal with their problems by what they see on TV, hear on the radio, or read on the Internet. You may want to show your group a few clips of a movie or TV show or have them bring in some samples of their favorite music. Take some time to talk about the stresses in the show or song. How do the characters deal with the stress? How does this affect their relationships with others or how they live their lives? How does this relate to your kids and the pressure in their lives?

PRECIOUS TO GOD

1. In your opinion, what is it that gives a human life **value**?

2. Take a look at **Psalm 8**. What is the question David (the author) asks in verse 4?

   What do you think that means?

3. David lists some of the awesome things God has done for his people. Explain each item below in your own words.

   a. God made us just one step lower than angels.

   b. God crowned us with glory and honor.

   c. God set us up as rulers over everything else on earth.

   d. God put us in charge of the earth's resources.

4. Check out **John 3:16**. This is a frequently quoted verse because of its message of salvation. Because of his great love for you, what did God do?

   What wonderful blessing do you receive?

   What does this tell you about how valuable you are to God?

   How would you explain this to people who don't think that they are loved by God?

5. Now turn to **Romans 8:31-32**. What three things in these verses show that God cares for you?

   Take a look at verses 35-39. Will God's love for you and the high value he places on you ever change? Why or why not?

6. How does being so valued by God make you feel?

   How does this change how you feel about God?

   Does this change how you feel about your life and how you live it?

PRECIOUS TO GOD [God's love for us—Psalm 8]

THIS WEEK

During this uncertain time in their lives, teenagers sometimes feel worthless—unloved and unappreciated by their peers, friends, teammates, and even their families. This TalkSheet gives your group a look at the high value that God places on each person. This value—which is found in God, not human merit—makes life worthwhile and meaningful.

OPENER

Have your group list several of the most popular songs on the radio. Write them on a whiteboard or on a poster board. Working together with your students, evaluate which songs either place value on a person (a love song, for instance) or seem to devalue people (songs that advocate violence, sexual assault, or substance abuse).

For the songs that value people, ask your students to determine why the singer values the other person—are these for good reasons or faulty ones? Is the person singing about true human love—or more about sexuality or outward appearance? You may want to have a few of them quote the lyrics if they can (you may be surprised at your kids' memories!) Rate each song on a scale of 1 to 10 (1 being "This song truly values an individual" and 10 being "This song disses everything about a person"). Have your students thought about the lyrics before? Be sure not to condemn your kids for the music they listen to, but do point out that many songs treat humans much differently than God treats them. Then point out that you'll be discussing the real reasons each person is valued and why each person's life is meaningful.

THE DISCUSSION, BY NUMBERS

1. The way your students answer this question will reveal their philosophies about life and their priorities. Some may have a hard time responding. Point out that each of them is an instrument to be used by God—each of them has value placed on them by God. Without this purpose, some people feel useless and hopeless. How valuable do your kids feel? Do they know that they are loved by God?

2. After your students have read the psalm, take some time to summarize its sections. The first part speaks of God's majesty, the second part finds David wondering how such a great God could care about mere humanity, and the third part lists some of the wonderful things God has done for us. You may want to have your group, or parts of it, rephrase each section in their own words. How do these sections apply to their lives?

3. Allow your students to express their thinking. How did they summarize each of these statements? Which one meant the most to your group?

4. By now your class members should be convinced that God places a very high value on each of them. Help them understand that because God values them, they're truly valuable—and their lives are meaningful! What makes them feel invaluable in today's society? How does this compare to how God feels about them? Who would they rather feel valued by—their peers or God?

5. Use this passage to point out that God's love is permanent—it doesn't change and it never goes away. Point out that God's love is based on his nature and not on what your kids do. It doesn't matter how much money they have, how popular they are, how good-looking they are, or what grades they get. God loves them and is willing to accept them into his kingdom and family if they accept his love and forgiveness.

THE CLOSE

Why should your kids value themselves and others? The answer is simple—because God does! Showing God's love to others means accepting others for who they are and valuing them, just as God does. Let your kids know that you value each of them! Now how do they value each other? Their friends? Their sometimes irritating parents? Their annoying siblings? You may want to close by praying for the members of your class, thanking God for demonstrating how much he values them—and asking for his strength to help them value others as he values them.

MORE

- Jesus showed his love for others as no one else ever has. Not only did he die for us, but he showed his love in his daily life on earth. You may want to have your kids look for examples in the Bible of how Jesus showed people that he valued them—hanging out with sinners, healing the lepers, and more. Talk about how your kids can reflect Christ in their own lives.

- Low-self-esteem robs people of the value they have in God. In order to love others and love God, people must love themselves, too! You may want to talk about self-esteem with your kids. What shapes their self-esteem? What influence does society have on them? Read Matthew 22:37-39 with your group. What does this say about loving ourselves as God loves us?

BEING A FOOL

1. Rate the following situations on a scale of 1-10, **1** being **most foolish to ignore** and **10** being **least foolish to ignore**.

___ A traffic signal at a busy intersection

___ What God says in the Bible

___ Advice from a college or career counselor

___ The school tardy bell

___ A strange-colored mole that suddenly appears on your skin

___ The oil warning light on your car

___ The coach's suggestions for your game

___ Health safety cautions, such as abstaining from sex to prevent getting an STD

___ Your curfew or rules given by your parents

___ The teacher's recommendation of what to study for the upcoming exam

2. Check out **Psalm 14**. What does the fool deny, according to verse 1?

Now read **Matthew 7:24-27**. What did the foolish man do in verses 26-27?

Why would that be the same as ignoring Jesus' words?

3. Is it possible to believe in God and give your life to him—but still ignore him? Why or why not?

4. Take a look at this list of paraphrases from the Bible about fools. How do you rate? Next to each item, write **T (That's me)**, **S (Sometimes me)** or **N (Never me)**.

___ A fool talks his way into trouble (Proverbs 10:8).

___ A fool gossips (Proverbs 10:18).

___ A fool takes pleasure in sin (Proverbs 10:23).

___ A fool ignores good advice (Proverbs 12:15).

___ A fool gets angry fast and gets in fights (Proverbs 12:16).

___ A fool lives a self-destructive life (Proverbs 14:1).

___ A fool doesn't care who gets hurt (Proverbs 14:9).

___ A fool is reckless (Proverbs 14:16).

___ A fool ignores parental discipline (Proverbs 15:5).

___ A fool wastes money (Proverbs 17:16).

___ A fool likes to blab uninformed opinions (Proverbs 18:2).

___ A fool doesn't save or plan for the future (Proverbs 21:20).

___ A fool is lazy (Ecclesiastes 4:5).

From *High School TalkSheets Psalms and Proverbs—Updated!* by Rick Bundschuh and Tom Finley. Permission to reproduce this page granted only for use in the buyer's own youth group. www.YouthSpecialties.com

BEING A FOOL [foolishness — Psalm 14]

THIS WEEK

What is a fool? According to Psalm 14:1, a fool is someone who believes there is no God. This TalkSheet will alert students to the dangers of ignoring God and being a fool—a mistake even Christians can make.

OPENER

What do your kids think a fool is? They may have many different ideas based on what they see on TV and in the movies. Ask them to list some examples of how people can be foolish. Is there a TV show or movie in which there's a foolish character? What did he or she do that was foolish? Was it the way the foolish character treated someone or something they did? You may want to make a list of these examples of foolishness. And add some ideas of your own if you want.

Maybe show a few clips of some TV shows, movies, or commercials. Point out that often the media uses foolish people to make something humorous. But sometimes the acts of foolishness are tragic. You may want to ask the group to name something foolish that they've done. What were the results? What lessons did they learn from their foolishness? Then jumpstart this discussion by pointing out that God has a different idea of what a fool is.

THE DISCUSSION, BY NUMBERS

1. Take some time to talk about your students' responses and let them suggest possible consequences of ignoring the various situations and God's Word. Point out that, while it's foolish to ignore most of these situations, ignoring the Bible is by far the worst.

2. In Psalm 14, God calls the one who denies him a fool. In Matthew 7:24-27 Jesus says that the person who ignores his words is a fool. Discuss the imagery that Jesus used—the lack of sure-footedness, the pressures, and the failure. Make sure students understand that it isn't just hearing Christ's words but obeying them that makes the difference.

3. Unfortunately, Christians ignore God, leading them into problems that could've been avoided. Do your students understand that making a habit of ignoring God is a sign of deep spiritual troubles? How often do they think they (or their friends) ignore God? Why is it easy or tempting to ignore him?

4. How did your kids answer these questions? Which of these problems are the most common among teenagers their age? Would a person who behaved in these ways be considered a fool by most teens? What is the opposite of each foolish action? Do you know people who set positive examples in these areas?

THE CLOSE

Close by pointing out the progression of foolishness—denying or ignoring God, disobeying God, and doing foolish things. You may want to talk with your group about what may be foolish things in their world. Going too far in a dating relationship? Drinking too much and trying to drive? Lying to a parent? So how can they avoid being a fool in God's eyes? Encourage them to start by opening up to him, spending time reading the Bible, and doing what it says. Remind them that it's not easy to live by the Bible every day—people are human, and humans mess up. Challenge them to evaluate how they stand in God's eyes at this point and what they need to do to get right with him.

MORE

● Do your kids need help getting motivated to do their devotions and spend time with God? Encourage your students to get into the Word by helping them to develop a reasonable Bible reading schedule. There are several devotionals available for high school students, as well as many useful Web sites with student links and devotionals, including www.christianteens.net or www.teens4god.com). Or consider doing a Bible study with them on a topic or issue that's real in their lives. Check out www.YouthSpecialties.com for information on small group and Bible study resources including *Good Sex, Creative Bible Lessons, Talking the Walk, Downloading the Bible,* and many more.

● Are your kids dealing with foolishness in their lives? Would they consider themselves foolish in some area of their life? If so, challenge your group members to think of one thing that they'd like to change or work on—maybe studying more, listening to their parents, re-evaluating a friendship or relationship, or something else. Encourage them to set a goal for themselves and to write it down. Then follow up with them via phone or e-mail to see how they are doing—you can encourage them and form a deeper relationship at the same time!

NOT SHAKEN

1. What would you like to have if you could **have it all**? Check out the list below and put an arrow by the **five traits** or **talents** that you'd most like to have.

   Great singing voice
   Perfectly straight, white teeth
   Extraordinary intelligence
   Drop-dead gorgeous looks
   Quick reading skills
   Bulging muscles
   Musical talent
   Good hand-eye coordination
   Poetic abilities
   A degree from a four-year college
   An exceptional memory
   Confident stage presence

   Sense of humor
   Lots of brains
   Strong, healthy bones
   Clear skin
   Athletic abilities
   Leadership ability
   Stamina
   Sexual appeal
   Knowledge of politics
   A charismatic personality
   All the right clothes
   Other—

2. From the list above, what do you think are the **five most important** traits to God?

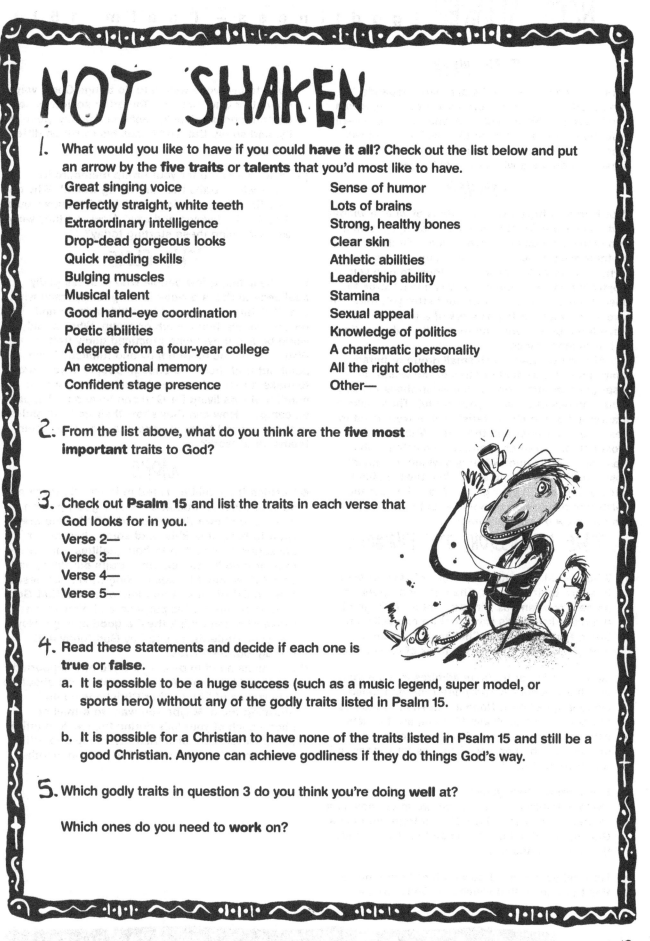

3. Check out **Psalm 15** and list the traits in each verse that God looks for in you.
   Verse 2—
   Verse 3—
   Verse 4—
   Verse 5—

4. Read these statements and decide if each one is **true** or **false**.
   a. It is possible to be a huge success (such as a music legend, super model, or sports hero) without any of the godly traits listed in Psalm 15.

   b. It is possible for a Christian to have none of the traits listed in Psalm 15 and still be a good Christian. Anyone can achieve godliness if they do things God's way.

5. Which godly traits in question 3 do you think you're doing **well** at?

   Which ones do you need to **work** on?

NOT SHAKEN [godliness—Psalm 15]

THIS WEEK

Sports heroes, Hollywood stars, music legends, supermodels, power brokers—are these people winners? God has his own idea of what a winner is—his definition is given in Psalm 15. This TalkSheet will teach your kids eleven attributes of godliness—those that define a winner in God's eyes.

OPENER

Your kids may have their own ideas of what a winner and a loser are. To start this discussion, split them into smaller groups (or have all them do this activity on their own). Give each small group or person a term—winner or loser—and ask them to give you an illustration of what one is. They can use words to describe the winner or loser—or better yet, they can give an example or tell as story of a winner or loser. Have them brainstorm and then write a description of the winner or loser.

Afterwards, have each small group or person share their description or story of the winner or loser (be sure that none of the illustrations include actual names of those in your group). Then make a master list of the characteristics that were used to describe the winner and the loser. What was the most common trait or characteristic listed? What was the most unique? What is a winner commonly associated with? Spend some time talking about each of these with your group. Then start out the TalkSheet discussion by pointing out that God has his own view of what a winner is.

THE DISCUSSION, BY NUMBERS

1. What would your students choose? Ask for some to share their answers. Then ask your group to name a few famous winners that have some of the traits listed. It's likely that no one will mention a Bible character. Challenge them on this point, and then ask them to think of one or two.

2. God has a list of traits he admires in a person, but they are considerably different than those listed in question 1. None in question 1 matches the godly traits of Psalm 15. Compare the lists with your group. What differences do they see and why are human specifications for winners different from God's?

3. This item will help your teens realize that the characteristics of a person the world defines as a winner are considerably different from the things God values. What questions do they have about these verses and traits?

4. How did your kids agree with these statements? Point out again that winning in God's eyes is

open to everyone willing to do things God's way—no matter who they are. Too often society bases worth on physical looks, abilities, money, popularity, and so on. But God bases his worth on different qualities.

5. Take some time for your group members to share which traits they are doing well at. Why do they think they are doing well? Which ones would they like to develop and why? How can they work on developing these starting today?

THE CLOSE

Close by listing a few people who possess godly qualities—perhaps a well-known public person who is a Christian or someone your kids admire and respect within their church or group. What would the world be like if everyone practiced godly traits? Would people be more happy and fulfilled? Then point out that there are enough people in your group to make a real difference at their schools! Just a handful of kids living for God can have a real impact on campus. How can they show their godly qualities to those around them at school, at home, on their teams, or at work?

MORE

- Besides the qualities listed in Psalm 15, there are several other characteristics of a godly person listed and shown throughout the Bible. You may want to have your kids read some chapters or passages in the Bible to find qualities and attributes or a godly winner. What traits did Paul possess? How about Moses or King David? Or Jesus? Make a list of these traits and point out that God uses everyone for his purpose and plan—even those who don't think they're good enough. How can your students be used by God today and throughout their lives?

- Christians need to be encouraged and supported by other Christians. You may want to talk aboutthe importance of lifting other Christians up and affirming them. Maybe you want to e-mail or phone each of your kids during the week to affirm them. Or let them pick their own people to affirm throughout the week and in the coming months.

COUNT YOUR BLESSINGS

1. What does the word **blessed** mean to you?

2. Which of the following do you think you are blessed with?

- ❑ Athletic ability
- ❑ Good looks
- ❑ Friends
- ❑ A house in a safe neighborhood
- ❑ Girlfriend or boyfriend
- ❑ Academic success

- ❑ Sense of humor
- ❑ Good parents
- ❑ Cheerful personality
- ❑ Ambition for the future
- ❑ A supportive family
- ❑ Positive outlook
- ❑ A special talent

- ❑ An after-school job
- ❑ Popularity
- ❑ Car or vehicle
- ❑ Health
- ❑ Lots of money
- ❑ Trendy clothes
- ❑ Other—

3. Where do think you fall on the following scale?

◆ ▮▮▮▮▮▮▮▮▮▮▮▮▮▮▮▮▮▮ ◆

I'm blessed more than most people • I'm blessed about the same as most people • I'm blessed less than most people

4. Check out **Psalm 16**. Starting with verse 5, find seven blessings and rewrite them in your own words below.

Verse 5—

Verse 5—

Verse 6—

Verse 10—

Verse 11—

Verse 11—

Verse 11—

5. Below is a list of blessings that God gives to Christians—these are all mentioned in Ephesians, a letter the apostle Paul wrote to the church at Ephesus. Where do you stand on each of these blessings? On each line, put a **B (blessing for me)**, **M (maybe a blessing for me)** or **N (not a blessing for me)**.

___ Before the world was even created God picked you out to enjoy him.

___ He adopted you as his child into his forever family.

___ He redeemed (purchased) you and forgave all your sins.

___ He saved you.

___ He gave you the Holy Spirit to live in your heart.

___ You have an inheritance (a place and a reward) in heaven.

___ You have access (through prayer) to the Almighty God.

COUNT YOUR BLESSINGS [being blessed—Psalm 16]

THIS WEEK

Teenagers need to hear and see adults like you expressing the joys, pleasures, and benefits of walking with God. David made a list of blessings for Christians when he wrote Psalm 16. As you go through it with your students, be sure to let them know what it is that makes this true for you—"my heart is glad and my tongue rejoices" (Psalm 16:9).

There are times when it's hard to feel happy or blessed—people, including teenagers, deal with a lot of challenges and difficulties. Be sensitive to problems in your kids' lives that may be overwhelming them.

OPENER

Start off by asking your kids to write their names on a piece of paper. Collect the papers and then have everyone pick a name of another person in the group. Be sure that no one gets his or her own name. Then ask them to write down a list of the blessings that they would list if they were the person on the list. What traits or qualities does that person have?

Have each person read the blessings that they listed for the other person. Or, if you don't feel comfortable doing that, ask them to give the list of blessings back to the person. Was it hard to list the blessings of another person? What was easy about listing the blessings of someone else? Is it easier or harder than listing one's own blessings? How does receiving the list of blessings make him feel? How do they feel knowing that God sees the same blessings in each person?

THE DISCUSSION, BY NUMBERS

1. What does the word *blessed* mean to your kids? Point out that in the Bible *blessed* most often means "happy" or "to be envied". Most people who are blessed are people in a happy, enviable position, and who realize it.

2. Your kids may not want to share what they think they're blessed with. That's okay. Point out that the lists in question 2 are things the world would consider good blessings. How does God view these blessings? How can these blessings turn negative if they're handled poorly?

3. How do your students rate themselves on this scale? Not everyone receives all of the blessings listed in item 2. Some people might have only a few or even none of them. But as your students will see in the next step, God does provide guaranteed blessings every believer can enjoy. And if you have any students who feel they've been left behind in the blessings department—God hasn't forgotten about them (as they'll soon see.)

4. Take some time to discuss each of these blessings and help your students relate these principles to their lives. Psalm 16 is just a tiny sample of the many Bible passages that speak of the gifts Christians can enjoy. What other blessings does the Bible mention?

5. The blessings of Psalm 16 are for all believers—regardless of looks, popularity, wealth, or whatever. What do these blessings and promises mean to your kids? How do these make them feel? And how do these blessings compare with those in item 2? Take time to answer any questions that your kids may have about these statements.

THE CLOSE

Point out that life isn't fair—not everyone is blessed equally by worldly standards. But everyone is loved by God and is blessed by him individually. You may want to lead the class in prayer, thanking God for each blessing you've talked about. Encourage your kids to form a habit of counting their blessings and thanking God daily for the goodness he shows them. Can they see his blessings in their lives?

MORE

● What does it take to receive God's blessings—and see the blessings in our lives? Point out that God isn't a distant being in the heavens—nope, he's a loving father who loves them and is active in their lives. How does prayer play a role in blessings? Does God answer prayers and bless some people more than others? You may want to talk about the ways that God answers prayer—with yes, no, or wait (maybe). What is God saying to your kids today? What issues is he telling them to wait on?

● You may want to make a Wall of Blessings with your group. Hang up a long piece of white roll-out paper on the wall and provide markers for your kids, magazines, and newspapers for your kids. Then let 'em go crazy by drawing pictures, pasting up photos, and writing words, verses, or other thoughts that describe the blessings they've received from God.

BRING IT ON!

1. List the **three most difficult** challenges that high school students face.

2. Check out **Psalm 20**. This passage lists a bunch of awesome promises for Christians. Make a list of these promises in your own words and pick the **three** that are most meaningful to you.

3. Pick one of the following situations and answer the questions below.
   a. Kerry likes to date—and she wants to keep her dating life wholesome and fun.
   b. Skye wants to lead her best friend to Christ.
   c. Alexis has decided to stay away from alcohol, but some of her friends drink—especially at parties.
   d. Juan, Drew, and Maria are best friends. Their school morale is at an all-time low due to violence, drugs, and the like—but these three friends want to work to improve things.

   What are the **most important steps** the person or persons must take to achieve the goal?

   What are things the person or persons must **not do** to achieve the goal?

   How can **God** help out at each step?

4. What is one **significant challenge** or **goal** in your life right now?

   What promises from **Psalm 20** can help you with this challenge or goal?

   How do you think God can help you walk through your challenge or meet your goal?

BRING IT ON! [facing challenges—Psalm 20]

THIS WEEK

Teenagers face significant challenges in their daily lives—some of which include temptations like drugs, sex, or depression. Others are dealing with split families, abusive relationships, or struggles in school. On the other hand, some challenges are positive, such as studying for good grades, replacing a bad habit with a good one, being part of an athletic team, or leading a friend to Christ.

In Psalm 20, David prayed for victory in battle. His prayer illustrates the best way to face any challenge—to have God on your side. This TalkSheet focuses on the challenges your kids face and how the God can—and does—work though their situations.

OPENER

Start off by showing some video clips of people who have faced challenges in their lives—a few recommended ones include *Changes* (www.walkingonwater.org) or *Real Kids* (www.YouthSpecialties.com). Follow up by asking for your kids' reactions to the videos. What did they feel or sense from the people portrayed? What struggles did they face and how did their faith play a role in their decisions or lifestyles?

Or read a story or illustration about someone who is facing a challenge or struggle. You may want to ask your students to bring in examples or illustrations of people that they've read about during the last week or month. Bank on them! They're bound to find stories or situations of people on the Internet, TV, or radio. Encourage them to bring examples of both Christians and non-Christians—for example, how would someone of a different religion deal with challenges?

THE DISCUSSION, BY NUMBERS

1. Make a list of the top few challenges common to many of your students. What are the most common? Which ones would they rate as most difficult? Why or why not?

2. Discuss each of these phrases, allowing students to suggest ways each thought relates to the subject of victory. (Sacrifices and burnt offerings speak of coming to God to be made right with him, trusting one's life to him, and desiring to surrender to him). Note the important ideas of praying to God, clinging to God, trusting in God, being right with God, and needing to have godly goals.

3. You can use the situations listed here—or simply talk about the top one or two challenges the students suggested in question 1. Point out that God helps people meet their challenges and goals in real ways. For example, he might help Kerry meet

a guy who will treat her with respect. God could cause Alexis to realize she might need to stay away from both the influence of her friends who drink and the parties that tempt her. There are many ways God can help a person face a tough challenge.

4. What challenges or goals do your kids have? What significant goal or challenge will they face this year? In two years? In five years? How can they make wise decisions and rely on God today?

THE CLOSE

Remind your group that everyone faces challenges and struggles—no matter what age or gender they are. How one deals with tough situations will affect how they handle decisions and challenges in the future. How are your kids going to deal with their tough times in their lives? Will they drink away their frustrations? Try to deal with them alone? Or will they let God step in and take action in their lives? Close by re-reading the promise of encouragement in Psalm 20 and a time of prayer for your kids and the goals, struggles, and challenges that are before them.

MORE

● The Bible is full of stories of victory. Split up your group into smaller groups to see what stories of victory they can find. There are several in the Old Testament as well as some in the New Testament. How would your kids classify victory? Is it simply winning a war—or is it something more than that?

● Encourage your group members to support each other. Let your students determine what they will pray for, when they will pray, how they can encourage people in tangible ways, what events to attend, and so forth. Maybe form an e-mail list or Web board, or find some other way for your kids to share their struggles and prayer requests with each other.

FOLLOWING THE LEADER

1. Who would you say is the **chief guide** through life for most high school students?

2. Check out **Psalm 23**. Under each of the predicaments below, write which verse from the psalm applies to the problem.
   a. John has no idea what he wants to do when he graduates. He's very worried about his future.

   b. Carly is only 16 and already she's stressed out—tons of schoolwork plus her job. She would feel very insecure if she tried to relax.

   c. Terrence was raised in a strong church, but his family doesn't go anymore. He has a million questions about God and no answers.

   d. Gabriella's mom is battling cancer, and her doctors say the outcome could go either way—no guarantee that she'll live and no guarantee that she'll die.

3. Check out **John 10:11-16**. What does this passage say sheep are supposed to do?

4. How good a follower are you? Read the following statements and check the box under the category that is true for you.

	Yup, that's me	No way, that's not me
I like to pray.	❑	❑
I lean on God for a lot of stuff.	❑	❑
I rarely worry—I'm a carefree person.	❑	❑
I'm trying hard to be a good Christian.	❑	❑
I like to do things my own way.	❑	❑
I like hanging out at youth group.	❑	❑
I get angry at God if things don't go right.	❑	❑
I ask my parents or other adults for advice.	❑	❑
I get really uptight about things.	❑	❑

5. Paraphrase your favorite verse from Psalm 23 by writing it in your own words. What is God saying to you through these verses?

FOLLOWING THE LEADER [following Christ—Psalm 23]

THIS WEEK

Some of your kids may think that Psalm 23 is only read at funerals—but it's actually a song for the living. It says exactly what your kids need to hear—that they have a guide, leading them and watching over them. These verses paint a picture of care and guidance that the Lord provides and that the world so desperately needs.

OPENER

Who do your kids look up to? Who do they admire or respect in society—either past or present? Make a list with your students of the people who your kids consider to be role models. They'll probably list athletes, world leaders, or others who have an influence on people. What do these people do that makes them worthy of admiration or respect?

THE DISCUSSION, BY NUMBERS

1. Who leads your kids though life? Make a list of the people they choose and ask them to explain what makes a good guide. Do non-Christians have different guides than Christians? Why or why not? Discuss the need for a guide in life, and talk about who the best guide really is.

2. Take some time to talk about these situations in light of Psalm 23. How realistic are these situations in the lives of your kids? How would your kids respond in these situations? You may want to give the group time to expand to other situations where Psalm 23 could give hope and encouragement.

3. Read this verse with your group and ask for some volunteers to share their answers. How does this verse apply to their lives today? Point out that to listen to Christ means to hear and obey—obedience is the key to following the Shepherd!

4. This gives your kids a chance to evaluate their spiritual strength. You may want to take a general poll of your group to see how they responded to these statements, instead of asking for specific responses. Would your kids like to change how they responded? If so, how can they begin to trust in and rely on God more?

5. Ask for a few volunteers to read their paraphrases. You may want to rewrite or paraphrase the whole psalm as a group. What's the greatest hope that your kids find from these verses?

THE CLOSE

Why do your kids think this psalm is most often read on sad occasions, such as funerals, or during hard times? Many of your kids may be facing "valleys" of their own. Take some time to talk about the frustration and despair that comes when facing challenges that seem impossible to overcome. Be sensitive to your group members—some of them may have lost parents, loved ones, or may be dealing with serious situations in their lives, such as abuse, alcoholism, depression, and more.

Encourage your students to pick one area from question 5 that they would like to improve in. What are they struggling most with in their lives? Then have them choose a verse from Psalm 23 that applies the area of needed improvement. Is it easy to follow and let God lead? Why or why not? Take some time to talk about the fears of human nature and what scares teenagers about completely following God.

You may want to read Hebrews 13:20-21 and close with a time of prayer with your group.

MORE

● You may want to ask some of your Internet-savvy kids to dig around and see what fun facts or information they can find about sheep—and also about shepherds (they'll learn a little history in the process). You will need to do some back-up research just in case. On a whiteboard or poster board, make a list of the qualities or attributes of sheep. What about shepherds? Why would David draw a parallel between humans and sheep, and God and a shepherd? What do your kids think?

● Psalm 23 is just one passage in the Bible that talks about God leading and guiding his people. You may want to split your kids into smaller groups and let them look for other passages that talk about God's promises of hope and direction. Make a list of the passages on a whiteboard or poster board. What was the situation of the writer as he wrote? How did God get him or her though the situation? And what can this passage say to your youth today?

THE PERFECT PARENT

Note: The term parent *here refers to all kinds of parenting adults—birth, step, foster, and guardian.*

1. Here's a list of problems teens can have with parents or guardians. Which ones do you think are the **worst**? Rank them in order, with **1** being the **worst**.

___ Watching parents divorce
___ Enduring verbal or psychological abuse
___ Being treated like a child
___ Being afraid to talk to parents about personal things
___ Experiencing the death of a parent

___ Being told you can't date
___ Having parents who don't love each other
___ Living with alcoholism or drug abuse
___ Enduring physical or sexual abuse
___ Getting no respect or trust

Which **three** you think are the **most common**? Put a ✔ beside these.

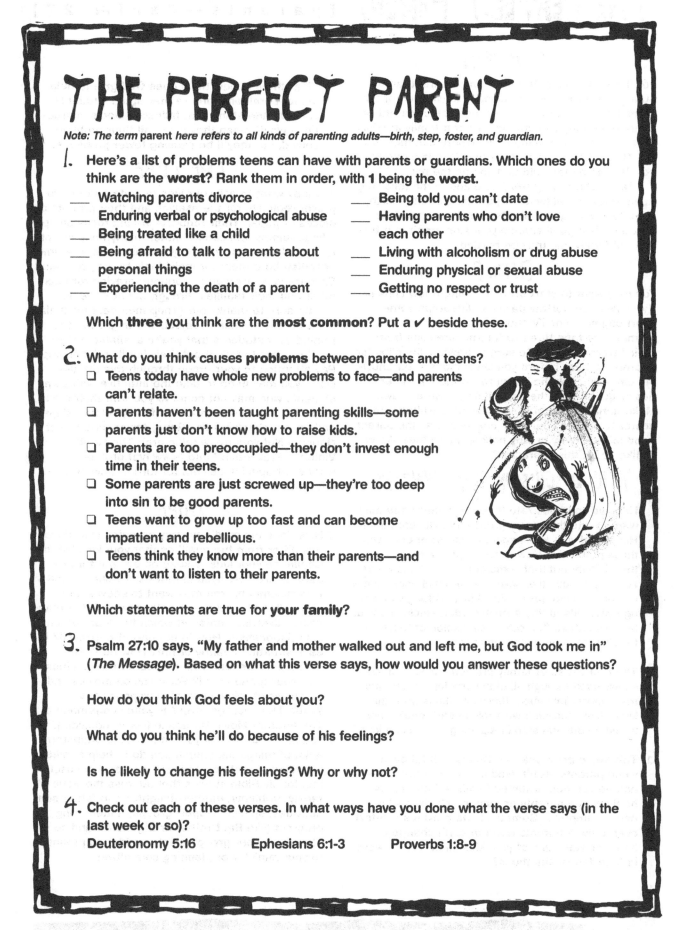

2. What do you think causes **problems** between parents and teens?
   ❑ Teens today have whole new problems to face—and parents can't relate.
   ❑ Parents haven't been taught parenting skills—some parents just don't know how to raise kids.
   ❑ Parents are too preoccupied—they don't invest enough time in their teens.
   ❑ Some parents are just screwed up—they're too deep into sin to be good parents.
   ❑ Teens want to grow up too fast and can become impatient and rebellious.
   ❑ Teens think they know more than their parents—and don't want to listen to their parents.

Which statements are true for **your family**?

3. Psalm 27:10 says, "My father and mother walked out and left me, but God took me in" (*The Message*). Based on what this verse says, how would you answer these questions?

How do you think God feels about you?

What do you think he'll do because of his feelings?

Is he likely to change his feelings? Why or why not?

4. Check out each of these verses. In what ways have you done what the verse says (in the last week or so)?
Deuteronomy 5:16   Ephesians 6:1-3   Proverbs 1:8-9

THE PERFECT PARENT [parents—Psalm 27]

THIS WEEK

For the first time in America, single-parent families outnumber two-parent families. And whether or not teens have one parent or two, or a foster parent or a guardian, they can still be part of a family in crisis. Kids are hurting in many ways. Where can they turn to? This TalkSheet discusses how God is a parent—how he can fill the void and soothe the pain.

Note: The term *parent* here and in the following items refers to all kinds of parenting adults—birth, step, foster, or guardian. Be sensitive to the fact that there's a good chance your kids aren't in a traditional family and may be hurting.

OPENER

You may want to start off by showing a few clips of TV shows that portray parents. Videotape some short segments of TV shows or ask your group members to tape three-to four-minute clips from their favorite shows. Be sure to preview the clips for appropriateness before you show them. After showing each clip, ask the group to list the characteristics or qualities of the parent(s) who were shown. Make a master list of their ideas on a whiteboard or poster board. In your kids' opinions, was the parent good or bad? Why or why not? What do they like or dislike about this character?

THE DISCUSSION, BY NUMBERS

1. How did your kids rate these problems? You may want to rate these as a group and talk about them. How could your kids begin to address or deal with these problems? How about helping a friend with them? Point out that some of the situations listed are very serious (i.e. sexual or verbal abuse)—some of which require professional help. Strongly encourage your kids to find a trusted adult—including you, fellow youth staff, a school counselor, or teacher—to talk with about these situations.

2. The root cause of family problems is sin, which shows itself through all of the problems listed and many more. Talk about these situations with your kids. How does sin have a role in each one? What would be the first step in repairing these situations?

3. This verse promises that God is faithful even when parents aren't. God loves your students—and he can help troubled families. Sometimes he'll change parents or teenage children who need to improve. Sometimes he provides comfort even though parents won't or can't change or improve. Have any of your kids seen God at work in their family situations?

4. What three suggestions does God give to help prevent problems before they start? Students should understand that following God's instructions won't mean they'll see all their problems solved, but they'll be causing fewer problems.

THE CLOSE

You may want to ask your kids to write one or two prayer requests for themselves and their parents on pieces of paper. Their requests should focus on specific problems and can be either anonymous or not. Collect all the slips and pray for them one at a time, or redistribute them for individuals to pray for aloud. Encourage your group to continue praying for each other and their families through the next week.

Be sure to thank your group members for their input on this stressful subject. You might want to remind your students that you're available if they need or want to talk about their family relationships. Pay attention to your group through this discussion—you may need to take the initiative with some students who may not come to you with their problems. For more information on family relationships and abuse, check out the Rape, Abuse, and Incest National Network (www.rainn.org), The Family Violence Prevention Fund (www.fvpf.org), or www.YouthSpecialties.com for further links and information.

MORE

● How does the media portray parents? How does this differ from the qualities that your kids listed? Challenge your kids to keep an eye out for how parents are portrayed in movies, TV shows, and in advertisements. You may want to show some other clips of movies—or gather some TV or magazine advertisements—in which there are parent-kid relationships. How is the parent portrayed? Is each situation healthy or not? How do these media parents rank with respect to the qualities that your group listed? For ideas on movies and TV shows check your local newspaper or visit Yahoo TV Coverage (http://tv.yahoo.com/main) or The Internet Movie Database (www.imdb.com).

● You may want to ask your students to brainstorm a list of things the church can do to help families, including parenting seminars, personal counseling, family Bible studies that address the issue of family problems, mother-daughter and father-son activities, special support groups, a mentoring program (like Big Brother or Big Sister) and so on. Then have your group select one idea to propose to your minister or planning committee.

STANDING IN AWE

1. What is your reaction to each of these phrases—**L (love it)**, **D (don't mind it)**, or **C (can't stand it)**.

    ___ Being a Christian
    ___ Talking to God
    ___ Talking about God
    ___ Sharing God's love with a friend
    ___ Attending these Bible discussions

    ___ Going to heaven
    ___ Serving God with my life
    ___ Learning more about God
    ___ Growing as a Christian
    ___ Loving God

2. Check out **Psalm 37:4** and answer the questions below.

    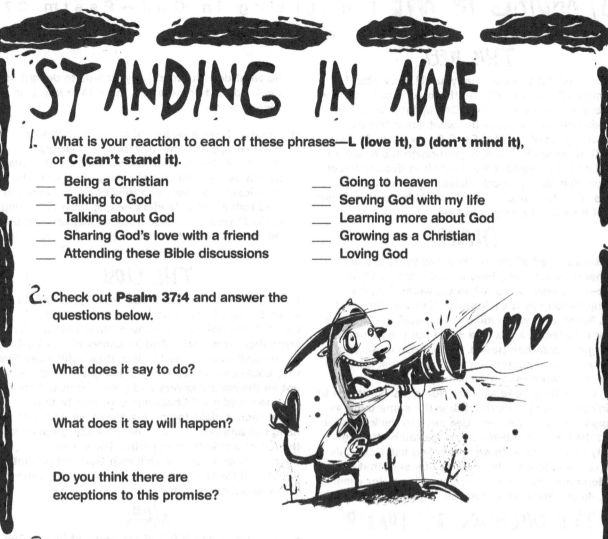

    What does it say to do?

    What does it say will happen?

    Do you think there are exceptions to this promise?

3. Check out **Psalm 37:4**. What do you think it means to delight in God? Think about your family, friends, school, or job—how could you delight in God in those areas?

4. Some people find it hard to delight in the Lord. They're too busy, too stressed out, or just don't know how to delight in God. List three things that you think would help a person delight in God, then list three things that might get in the way of delighting in God.

    What are some ways that you can delight in God?

    What do you need to change in your life that may be keeping you from delighting in him?

STANDING IN AWE [delighting in God—Psalm 37]

THIS WEEK

Jesus said, "If you love me, you will obey what I command" (John 14:15). Youth workers, parents, and teachers teach kids to love God by faithful acts of obedience and service—but what about the emotional aspect of love for God? Do your kids feel love for God, or do they simply go through the motions? Psalm 37:4 is perhaps the best short description of a heartfelt love for God—delighting oneself in the Lord. This TalkSheet will get your kids thinking about what it means to delight in God.

OPENER

Grab your kids' attention! You may want to start off by handing out something that you know they'll love—brownies, pizza, whatever works for your group as long as it's a surprise they aren't expecting. Right after you hand out the goods (or tell them your surprise) ask them to shout out the thoughts going through their heads. Write these down on a white board or poster board. Keep this list up for reference later on in the discussion.

Or if you want to skip the treats, ask your kids to think of all the words that mean the same thing as happiness or excitement. Get them to think of words that they hear in movies or on the radio—they're likely to come up with an interesting list. Keep this list up for reference later on and be sure that you understand the words before moving on (for example, do you know what "stoked" means?)

THE DISCUSSION, BY NUMBERS

1. This activity will force your kids to evaluate their delight factor—what were their responses to each item? Why did they have the reactions that they did? Which ones were positive or negative? And why did some have different reactions than others?

2. How did the group answer these questions? You may want to read this verse from some different versions of scripture to see the difference in how it is worded. Which one makes the most sense to your group?

   Be certain that everyone knows that the promise of receiving the desires of their hearts doesn't mean they can have anything they want any time they want! Delighting doesn't mean instant gratification! And it doesn't mean getting things their own way. God knows what people want and he gives Christians the object of their desires. He also places his godly desires in their hearts first. What happens when God's desires are different from what your kids want? How can they tell the difference between their own desires and God's?

3. So what does it mean for your kids to delight in the Lord? Jot some of the insights or ideas on a white board.

4. You may have a variety of answers to this one. Positive suggestions may include answered prayers, worship, fun Bible studies, or quiet meditation. Are the students' positive suggestions practical? If so, how can they begin to delight in God today? What hinders people from delighting in God? How can these become obstacles in their relationship with God? And what can they do to clear some of these out of their lives?

THE CLOSE

Point out that the reason God wants your kids to delight in him is because he loves them beyond belief. God created each one of them unique—he knew them from birth. And he knows what's best for them—and even wants to bless them with more than they could ask for. So why not delight in God? He's got all the right answers and gives the best direction anyone could give! Challenge your kids to think about their delight factor. Are they taking time to hang out and enjoy God or not? Finally, go back to the list of words from the intro. These words describe how it feels to chill with God and delight in him. But it takes effort on their part, too. Are they ready to delight in him?

MORE

- The Bible is chock full of examples of things God has done to delight his people. You may want to split your group up into smaller groups and ask them to find as many examples of God's greatness as they can. What names and titles of God can they find that describe his power and awesomeness? Did the people find delight in God? Which Bible characters gave praise to God—and why?

- Delighting in God means finding joy in him. What does it mean to have joy? How can a person tell if another is filled with joy? Have your kids ever found joy in God? You may want to ask for examples of how your students (or you, or your youth leaders) have found joy in God. What did he do for you that thrilled you? What did they or you learn from this experience?

TAKING IT WITH YOU

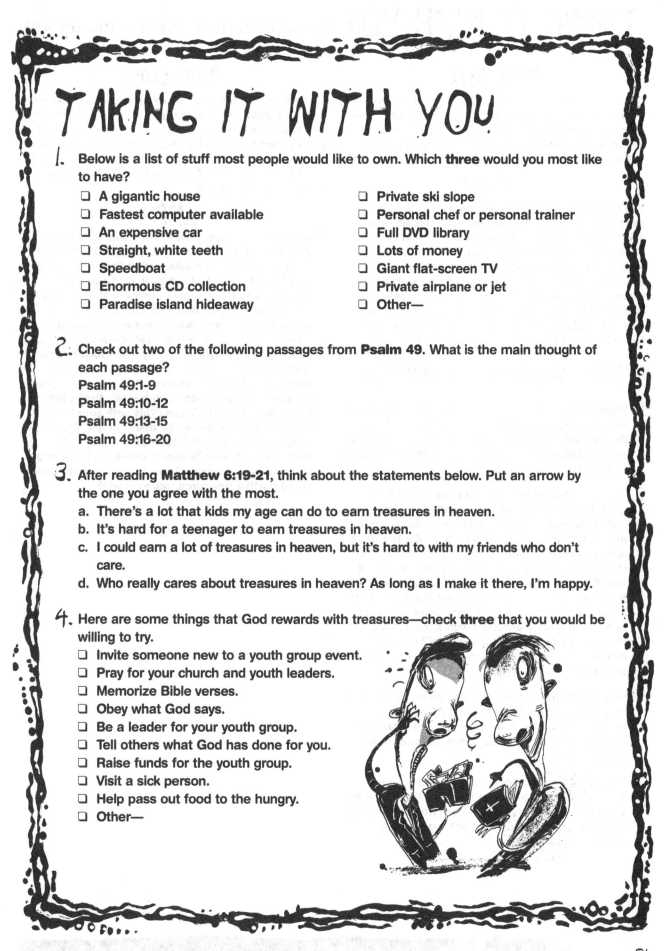

1. Below is a list of stuff most people would like to own. Which **three** would you most like to have?

   - ❑ A gigantic house
   - ❑ Fastest computer available
   - ❑ An expensive car
   - ❑ Straight, white teeth
   - ❑ Speedboat
   - ❑ Enormous CD collection
   - ❑ Paradise island hideaway

   - ❑ Private ski slope
   - ❑ Personal chef or personal trainer
   - ❑ Full DVD library
   - ❑ Lots of money
   - ❑ Giant flat-screen TV
   - ❑ Private airplane or jet
   - ❑ Other—

2. Check out two of the following passages from **Psalm 49**. What is the main thought of each passage?
   Psalm 49:1-9
   Psalm 49:10-12
   Psalm 49:13-15
   Psalm 49:16-20

3. After reading **Matthew 6:19-21**, think about the statements below. Put an arrow by the one you agree with the most.
   a. There's a lot that kids my age can do to earn treasures in heaven.
   b. It's hard for a teenager to earn treasures in heaven.
   c. I could earn a lot of treasures in heaven, but it's hard to with my friends who don't care.
   d. Who really cares about treasures in heaven? As long as I make it there, I'm happy.

4. Here are some things that God rewards with treasures—check **three** that you would be willing to try.
   - ❑ Invite someone new to a youth group event.
   - ❑ Pray for your church and youth leaders.
   - ❑ Memorize Bible verses.
   - ❑ Obey what God says.
   - ❑ Be a leader for your youth group.
   - ❑ Tell others what God has done for you.
   - ❑ Raise funds for the youth group.
   - ❑ Visit a sick person.
   - ❑ Help pass out food to the hungry.
   - ❑ Other—

TAKING IT WITH YOU [treasures in heaven—Psalm 49]

THIS WEEK

What are treasures in heaven? It sounds confusing, especially since people can't take their earthly possessions with them. This TalkSheet talks about heavenly treasures and how your kids can start to build up these rewards in heaven starting today.

OPENER

You may want to start off asking your kids to list expensive material possessions that people own—such as limousines, yachts, mansions, and planes. Make a list of their responses on a poster board or whiteboard. Now ask the group which ones of these would be considered treasures in heaven. Your group may be confused! Point out that people can't take earthly riches with them to heaven—but they can earn riches in heaven that will never go away. Not a bad way to invest in the future, eh?

THE DISCUSSION, BY NUMBERS

1. What makes each of these items valuable? What makes them so important or nice to have? Why do your kids think Christians put so much emphasis on material things, yet don't work just as hard to build up treasures in heaven?

2. The main thoughts you want your students to uncover are (1) that earthly wealth can't buy eternal life (verses 1-9); (2) wealth and life on earth are temporary (verses 10-12); (3) all die but there is hope in God's redemption (verses 13-15); and (4) nothing can be taken into eternity (verses 16-20). The sum total of the psalm is that material possessions are no substitute for the eternal life that God offers. In short, having things on earth is nice but having life in heaven is everything. How does that make your kids feel? Does it change their perspective of life on earth? Why or why not?

3. Which statements did your kids agree with? What makes it hard for them to build up heavenly treasures? What can be easy about it? Point out that God has no age requirements for earning treasures in heaven.

4. Ask for a few volunteers to share their answers. Then encourage everyone to follow through with one or more of these in the next week or month. Challenge them to set a realistic goal for a heavenly treasure.

THE CLOSE

Close by reminding your group that serving God isn't just for building up treasures in heaven—it's showing him that they love him. God sees the heart of each person and he can tell if their motives are honest and genuine. Challenge them to take their eyes off earthly things and to focus on how God can use them for his purposes.

MORE

● In terms of money, how rich do your kids think they are—in heavenly treasures, that is? Do they think they have the equivalent of $1 in earthly treasures? Ten bucks? More than that? Have they already earned heavenly treasures? Why or why not? What's helpful about comparing money to heavenly treasures? What's not good about it? Does it affect the way they feel about serving God?

● If God loves everyone equally—and forgives everyone's sin—then why would some people have more treasures than others? Why are some people going to be higher up in heaven than others? Take some time to discuss this with your kids. Some may be bothered by this thought. Also check out Matthew 5:3-12, Matthew 5:18-20, Matthew 6:20, and Matthew 18:1-4, and talk about these with your group. Does it help them understand earthly treasures more clearly?

HANG IN THERE

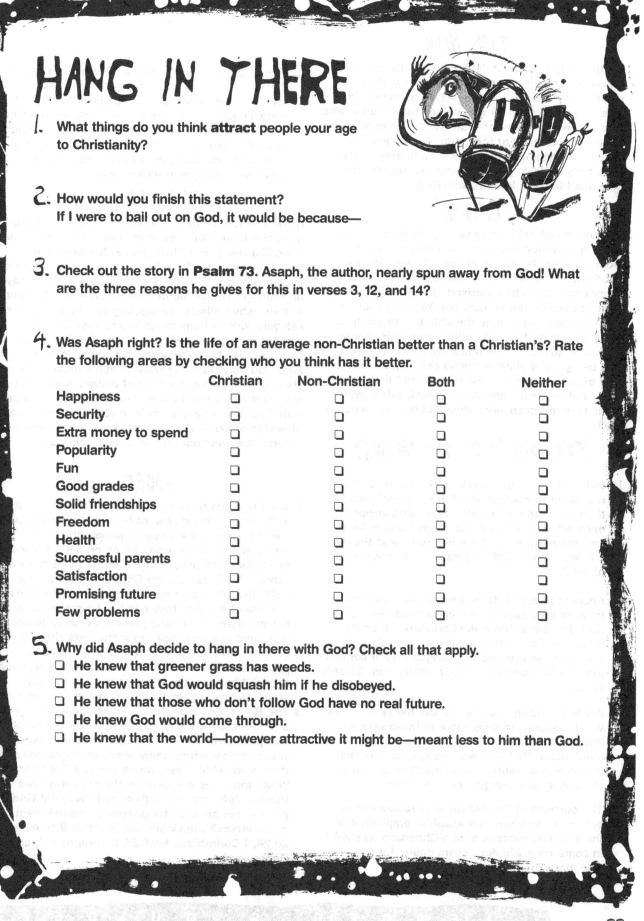

1. What things do you think **attract** people your age to Christianity?

2. How would you finish this statement?
   If I were to bail out on God, it would be because—

3. Check out the story in **Psalm 73**. Asaph, the author, nearly spun away from God! What are the three reasons he gives for this in verses 3, 12, and 14?

4. Was Asaph right? Is the life of an average non-Christian better than a Christian's? Rate the following areas by checking who you think has it better.

	Christian	Non-Christian	Both	Neither
Happiness	❑	❑	❑	❑
Security	❑	❑	❑	❑
Extra money to spend	❑	❑	❑	❑
Popularity	❑	❑	❑	❑
Fun	❑	❑	❑	❑
Good grades	❑	❑	❑	❑
Solid friendships	❑	❑	❑	❑
Freedom	❑	❑	❑	❑
Health	❑	❑	❑	❑
Successful parents	❑	❑	❑	❑
Satisfaction	❑	❑	❑	❑
Promising future	❑	❑	❑	❑
Few problems	❑	❑	❑	❑

5. Why did Asaph decide to hang in there with God? Check all that apply.
   ❑ He knew that greener grass has weeds.
   ❑ He knew that God would squash him if he disobeyed.
   ❑ He knew that those who don't follow God have no real future.
   ❑ He knew God would come through.
   ❑ He knew that the world—however attractive it might be—meant less to him than God.

HANG IN THERE [spiritual stamina—Psalm 73]

THIS WEEK

It's not easy to be a Christian. It sometimes seems easier for people to throw in the towel and do what's easy—to live for themselves as the world tells them to. Psalm 73 was written by someone who was experiencing a near-fatal crisis of faith because he stopped to gaze at the world around him. But despite everything, Asaph was able to stay on track. His words will give your students the ammunition they need to hang in there with God.

OPENER

You can launch this discussion by asking your students to describe the best times they've ever had. Most will probably speak of special trips, parties, good times with friends, or some other significant experience. You'll be surprised—few (if any) will cite Bible studies or church services. You may want to point this out—that while the Christian experience certainly has its fun and exciting moments, it also has more quiet, serious times. Some people think that being a Christian is always exciting, like some kind of radical religious experience. But that's not true. God wants his people to be still, listen, and focus on him—even when they feel like giving up on it all.

THE DISCUSSION, BY NUMBERS

1. How did your group answer this question? You may want to make a list of the suggestions and then ask students to rate the holding power of each attraction. Are these things likely to keep someone interested for a lifetime—or is the person who clings to them just going through a phase?

2. Encourage your kids to think about what causes them to lose interest in their commitment to God. Point out that while Christianity attracts a lot of people, some also wander away from it. Challenge your group to strengthen their commitment to God and shield their hearts from Satan's schemes.

3. Are these three reasons are still the same today? What reasons did Asaph give in these verses? Point out that verse 14's reference to punishment didn't mean that God was being cruel, but that Asaph was suffering some long-term problem such as illness, poverty, or depression.

4. The purpose of this activity isn't to see who is better, but to show that Asaph's complaint over the seeming success of non-Christians was valid. In some ways life does seem easier for non-Christians, but is it really?

5. The only untrue statement is that he was afraid God would squash him. It was Asaph's insight into the true nature of the unbeliever's plight, his knowledge that God would eventually glorify him, and his love for God that kept him on the straight road. Go over these reasons carefully with your group, helping everyone to privately evaluate their own strength in these areas.

THE CLOSE

Draw a simple picture of a temple on a white board or poster board. Be sure to include a front door and a smaller back door. Have your kids examine the temple (sanctuary) for a few seconds. Who are those in your group that are at the front door? Some may be waiting to enter. Some have been inside for quite a while, while others are slipping out the back door. Ask your kids to think about where they are in the sanctuary. Are they ready to enter? Do they know God already? Or do they want to get away from him? You may want to review Asaph's reasons for sticking with God in the face of distractions. Then give your kids some time to evaluate where they are with God. You may want to lead your kids in a time of prayer or worship and invite those who haven't entered the sanctuary to meet God right now.

MORE

● What reasons do people give for not wanting to be a Christian? You may want to ask your kids to pursue this question with some people this week. Encourage them to probe on an on-line chat room or to ask some people at the store, at work, or at school. Are these people Christians? If no, why not? Have they ever thought about it? Why or why not? Point out that they need to be prepared to explain their beliefs and present Jesus to them. At your next meeting, have your students share the answers that got on the whiteboard or poster paper. What answers make sense? Which of these don't? What counter-arguments do you or your students have against some of these answers?

● The Bible describes the Christian life as a race—a long-distance venture requiring determination and perseverance. Ask your kids to check out the verses below (either individually or in groups) and then write what it said about being a Christian. What analogies are given in these verses? Are these helpful for your kids or not? Why did God paint these pictures for people on earth? Want more verses? Check out Ecclesiastes 9:11, Acts 20:24, 1 Corinthians 9:24-27, 2 Timothy 4:7, and Hebrews 12:1.

SERVING THE SLUMS

1. Check out **Psalm 82:3-4**. Then in your own words, define these words from the passage.
   Defend—
   Maintain—
   Rescue—
   Deliver—

2. How do you think most people your age would react if they saw someone who was lonely, defenseless, or otherwise hurting? Put an arrow by the reactions that you expect would occur.

Just watch	Pray	Laugh at them
Feel bad	Tell someone	Gossip about them
Say something	Comfort them	Offer friendship
Defend them	Feel nothing	Blame them
Walk away	Talk to them	Help if it wasn't too hard
		Help even if it was hard

   Now think about the **three** that are your usual reactions to a situation like this. How do you think God would respond to your reaction?

3. What are some ways you could help the people below?
   a. Jasmine has a fairly severe speech impediment. People can't understand her easily, so she's usually ignored—or laughed at.

   b. Diante's dad is dying of cancer, and he's afraid of losing him, although he doesn't show it.

   c. A drunken man asks you for money for a meal.

   d. The gothic kid is being shoved around by gang members again.

4. A strong, single young man who refuses to work (because he can live off food stamps and rent subsidy) wants to borrow some bucks. Would you give him money?

   Why or why not?

SERVING THE SLUMS [helping others—Psalm 82]

THIS WEEK

The down and out include the hungry, the homeless, the lonely, the misfits—anyone who doesn't fit in with the crowd. They can be found in cities, suburbs, and (yes!) even high schools. This TalkSheet will guide your students toward their obligation to help in some way those who the world would rather ignore.

OPENER

Start off by lining five or six volunteers against one wall. All they have to do is move to the other side of the room together—except one of the volunteers can't use any body part except one arm! No walking, no crawling—but this person is welcome to drag himself by the arm! Give no other rules or details. Give a go signal and watch what happens. (Call time in 30 seconds or so.)

Most likely everyone made it across but the person with only one good arm. Point out that the best solution would have been for the other people to carry that person to the other side of the room! Did the group think of that? Or were they thinking only of themselves? Introduce the session by explaining that the discussion centers on people in need and ways your students can help them.

THE DISCUSSION, BY NUMBERS

1. Discuss the words, pointing out that these are things Christians are called to do. To *defend* means to protect, guard, and prevent injury or destruction. To *maintain* means to keep, hold, support, and preserve. To *rescue* is to free, save, liberate, and deliver. To *deliver* means the same as rescue and also has the idea of transport, as in taking a weak person away from a bad situation.

2. Which reactions are usual for teenagers? Why are these the common reactions? Are these the same ways that adults would respond? And how about Jesus—how would he respond to these situations?

3. You can have small groups work on one or two situations each. Allow time for each to reach a consensus about what should be done. If a group thinks the drunken man shouldn't be helped with money that he is likely to misuse, encourage your students to think more creatively. How can they offer him food, shelter, or clothing without giving cash?

4. This one may cause some heated debate. Your kids may be interested to know that the Bible says people who refuse to work shouldn't be fed (2 Thessalonians 3:10). What are some ways that your students could help the young man change his attitude? What alternative solutions would they have for this situation?

THE CLOSE

Encourage your students to take seriously God's call to help those who are in need. Skid Row isn't the only place where there are needy people—there're people in need everywhere. Challenge your group to not just feel bad for someone who is hurting, but to have the courage to get involved in practical applications of God's love.

MORE

● Put your kids on the other side! You may want to find a safe vacant lot somewhere and provide cardboard, scrap lumber, and plastic tarps out of which your students can make shelters for the night. Allow no food and provide no assistance (but of course make sure they're safe). Afterward debrief with your students about their night of homelessness. Did it change the way they think about the needy? How? What does it make them thankful for?

● You may want to brainstorm a practical way to share God's love with those in need in your community. With your group, come up with a unique service venture—something that your group can do to show God's love to others. Maybe collect and hand out used Bibles, serve free hot chocolate on a cold night, or some other way of reaching out. Your group might find that the most simple ways of serving can impact someone in a big way.

HEAVY-DUTY LOVE

1. Read **Matthew 5:43-44**. Where would you rate yourself on the scale below? Jesus said to love our enemies. To me loving people I don't like is—

◆ ▮▮▮▮▮▮▮▮▮▮▮▮▮▮▮▮▮▮▮▮▮▮ ◆

Absolutely impossible   **Always easy**

2. Here are three words in the Bible that are often translated as "love".

   Agape—God's perfect love.
   Eros—Romantic love or lust.
   Phileo—Brotherly love and friendship.

   For each of the phrases below associated with love, place an initial for one of the biblical types of love (**A, E or P**).

   ___ Valentine's Day   ___ Sharing a sandwich
   ___ Family reunion   ___ Feeding the hungry
   ___ Marriage   ___ Praying for an enemy
   ___ Birthday present to sister   ___ Forgiving someone you don't like
   ___ Donations to charity   ___ Infatuation
   ___ Christmas presents   ___ Flowers for a girlfriend
   ___ An encouraging e-mail   ___ A date
   ___ Jesus' death on the cross   ___ Helping a stranger

3. Look at **Matthew 5:43-44** again. Put a mark on the scale below to describe the sort of love Jesus is talking about.

◆ ▮▮▮▮▮▮▮▮▮▮▮▮▮▮▮▮▮▮▮▮▮ ◆

Action-oriented   **Feeling-oriented**
(Feelings of love not required)   (Feelings of love necessary)

4. Based on what you've read so far, give a one-sentence definition of **agape love,** the kind with which you can love an enemy.

5. Check out **Psalm 103:1-18.** You'll find a ton of examples of the many ways God loves you. List four in your own words.

HEAVY-DUTY LOVE [Christian love—Psalm 103]

THIS WEEK

Do your kids know that there are different kinds of love? This TalkSheet will give you and your group a chance to discuss some of the differences between God's love, brotherly love, and romantic love. And they'll learn that it's readily possible for Christians to display God's love in concrete ways.

OPENER

Start off by asking your students to describe the greatest act of love that they've ever witnessed. Who is the most loving person they know? Give some the chance to share stories or examples of those who've shown great love. Then ask the group to think of one-word descriptions for both the acts of love and the loving individuals they mentioned. You'll probably hear answers like *selfless*, *giving*, *generous*, and the like. Then mention that those are the same words that describe the love you're about to discuss—God's love.

Or you may want to pass around a dictionary or two and let volunteers each read one of the listed definitions for love. You may want to ask some to find definitions of love on the Internet and bring those in. Or have them define love in their own terms and then see what the dictionary has to say. There may be a variety of definitions and ideas. Jot these definitions on the whiteboard or poster board. Then launch the discussion by pointing out that you'll be looking together at love from God's perspective, which is found in the Bible.

THE DISCUSSION, BY NUMBERS

1. Some may have different ideas or opinions, based on their perception of the type of love Jesus was talking about. Point out that doing an act of love for someone (even an enemy!) is simply a matter of the will. Love is a choice, not necessarily a feeling toward someone.

2. Have your students vote on and discuss how emotions of love (or lack of them) are related to each item on the list. Some (like Valentine's Day) have more feelings involved. Your students will see that agape love isn't an emotion, but an act of will.

3. Where on the scale did the marks fall? How did your kids understand the verse in relation to this scale? Take a group consensus and ask why some answered as they did. How important are feelings and emotions when trying to show love to someone?

4. How did your kids define agape love? Ask for a few to share their definitions and then point out that that expressing God's love means choosing to do the right thing for someone in need.

5. You may want to assign verses 1-5, 6-10, and 11-18 to different groups of teens. Have students share their results. Point out that the things God has done for them illustrate agape love. God does these things for people even though we don't deserve them. God's acts of love are also examples of how Christians can show love to others.

THE CLOSE

The world's perception of love is so different from what God intended love to be. Society and the media have portrayed love as purely emotional and sexual. Take some time to point that out. What misconceptions of love have your kids seen or experienced? How do these differ from what God intended them to be? What are some examples in the Bible of people showing true love to others? You may want to look at a few illustrations of how Jesus showed love to others. His love is exactly the kind that Christians can model.

Encourage your group to evaluate their "love life." How are they doing in God's eyes? Are they showing agape love to those around them? Why or why not? Challenge them to think about what they can do to kick it in gear and start reflecting God's love to those in need around them.

MORE

● Try a love raid or war! Gather part or all of your group to surprise one of your students, pastor, or someone else in your church. Make sure you get the permission you need (from parents or whomever) and then have fun! Possibly cheer a member of your youth group's sports team or show up where one of your kids' place of employment (at the hot dog stand, in the mall!) Be creative and have fun showing love and encouragement.

● Take some time to analyze the different perceptions of love with you group that society and the media has. You may what to show a few movie clips or play a few popular songs. What does each say or show about what love means? How is this mentality helpful or harmful to people? What do they think Jesus would say about the movie clips if he were standing right by your group, watching or listening?

JUSTICE FOR ALL

1. Check out **Psalm 106:3**. According to this verse, what should you do to be blessed?

2. Now check out **Psalm 146:7-9**. Rewrite the passage in your own words—and replace the words and phrases (*the oppressed* and *the hungry*) with the word *me* (or your own name).

3. If you had the chance to set **one** of these wrongs right, what would you do? How could you change the situation to make it better?

   a. A little kid gets shoved out of line behind you.

   b. You learn that several students have answers to the midterm exam.

   c. One of your friends is being sexually abused.

   d. You witness someone you know shoplifting.

   e. A friend is injured by a drunk driver.

   f. Your teacher yells and is rude in class.

   g. You know that a classmate has stolen a gun.

   h. A fellow teammate drops hints about doing drugs.

4. Which statement below best describes your thoughts about **justice**?
   - ❑ Nobody said life would be fair.
   - ❑ I've experienced injustice in my own life.
   - ❑ Today's discussion has helped me understand a bit more.
   - ❑ Most injustices can't be fixed, so why try?
   - ❑ People should stop whining and face facts.
   - ❑ I'm ready to right the wrongs I see.
   - ❑ Christians should fight for justice.
   - ❑ I never really thought about justice before.

5. According to Jesus in **Luke 18:1-8**, what is the believer's secret to receiving justice?

JUSTICE FOR ALL [justice—Psalm 106, 146]

THIS WEEK

Teenagers today know enough to know they live in an unfair world. They certainly experience injustice on a self-centered level—some have better families than others; some get better grades. Others have virtually no problems, while some are flooded with serious issues in their lives. But teens also are sensitive to the injustices they see in the world. This TalkSheet will tap into that sensitivity and discuss God's call for them to maintain justice (Psalm 106:3).

OPENER

Newspapers and some magazines are filled with reports of injustice. Start off by splitting your group into smaller groups and distributing different sections of a newspaper (or magazines) to each group. You may want to get several newspapers from different towns (if you can). Ask each group to find three examples of injustices that are taking place in the world today. They can be situations of war, crime, unfair treatment, or anything else they think would qualify as an injustice. You may want to have each group share their findings with the group— what were the injustices? Where in the world are they taking place? Which ones hit home to your kids the most? Are some more serious than others? Have your kids thought about injustice before, or is it simply a fact of life?

THE DISCUSSION, BY NUMBERS

1. Talk about what being blessed means. What sort of blessings would a person who practices justice receive? Why does God address injustice in the Bible? Why would Christians be called to set the wrongs right—is it their problem to try?

2. How do your kids interpret this verse? You may want to ask a few to share their rewrites. Point out that God can use each of them to help right the wrongs—he's called them to do it and he will use them!

3. Some of these are tough situations to help right. Unfortunately, some of your kids may be dealing with these injustices. For each item, let your kids share their suggestions. Are these realistic ways of trying to help? Are there certain situations that your kids can't help right? Why or why not? What other situations have they thought of that aren't on this list?

4. What are your kids' thoughts on injustice? Have they actually thought about it before? Ask for a few volunteers to share their thoughts on injustice and why they chose the answer they did.

How does society in general respond to injustice? What about someone who is dealing with injustice in their own life?

5. The answer is prayer—it's the key to receiving justice. But it doesn't guarantee that Christians will have the easy road in life. Point out that God listens to prayers—and responds to them. It may take years for a prayer to be answered. But God gives peace and perseverance. How do your kids respond to this verse? What hope does if give them? How realistic is it for them to pray about serious issues, such as abuse or rape? Encourage your kids to be warriors through prayer—they can make a difference through prayer, whether they see it or not.

THE CLOSE

Point out that striving for justice is an action. It's faith on wheels. It isn't enough for Christians to feel sorry for people who are dealing with unfair situations. Christians must act—they're the ones who bring God's justice and mercy to hurting people. They are Christ in the flesh because they have Christ in their hearts. Are Christians striving for justice in today's world? Why or why not? What differences are they making? Take some time to pray with your kids about the injustices discussed in the introduction and how your kids can play a role.

MORE

● What does Jesus have to say about injustice? What does he say through his life and actions? He hung out with people who were facing injustice, including lepers, outcasts, and the sinners of the day. Check out a few examples of these with your kids and talk about his acts of achieving justice. He even defied the Sabbath law for justice (Matthew 12:10-11, Luke 13:14-15, John 5:18, John 9:14-16). What can your kids do in today's society to strive for justice?

● What is the cause of injustice in the world? Obviously sin is the culprit. Even Christians face injustices and deal with the effects of sin. Why do your kids think God commands Christians to act for justice? How should your kids respond to movies or music that promote injustice (for example, rap music that has violent and harmful lyrics)? Is there an injustice that you and your kids can act on? Tangible activities include writing letters to congressional or state representatives, speaking out on an issue, or approaching someone who is causing injustice. Challenge your kids to get acting this week—and seeing how God can use them.

FEAR NOT!

1. What's the difference between **worry** and **concern**?

2. Below are some possible teenage worries. Put a **C** next to the ones a person would have some sort of **control over** and an **NC** for those one would have **little** or **no control** over.

___ Dying
___ Getting acne
___ Parents divorcing
___ Living with alcoholic parents
___ Flunking a test
___ Having stress
___ Being unpopular
___ Being a victim of school violence
___ Being in a car accident

___ Breaking up
___ Enduring parental abuse
___ Living through a war
___ Not making a sports team
___ Being pressured to succeed
___ Getting in trouble with the police
___ Dating
___ Abusing drugs and alcohol
___ Becoming pregnant

If problems can be prevented or dealt with in some way, why do teenagers still worry about them?

3. If you had absolute control over the troubles above, would you still worry? Why or why not?

4. Check out **Psalm 112:7-8.**
What does it say about a godly person?
❑ A godly person never has problems.
❑ God will solve all my problems before any real damage is done.
❑ I don't have to fear problems even when they come.
❑ Problems will come, since it talks about triumph coming at the end.

5. You're talking to a friend who is worried about a situation. Using Romans 8:28, Philippians 4:6-7, and 1 Peter 5:7, what advice would you have for him or her? Would your advice change if this person is a Christian? Why or why not?

FEAR NOT! [fear — Psalm 112]

THIS WEEK

Trusting in God helps teenagers free themselves from the things that cause them anxiety—the fears of embarrassment, of being unpopular, not being attractive, bad grades, and a myriad of other things. This TalkSheet allows your class members to discuss their fears without fear and shows them how trust in God can cancel worry.

OPENER

What scares your teenagers today? What would they be most hesitant to talk about with you, their peers, or their parents? What subjects would make them the most nervous and scared? Or are your kids just so bold that they're not scared of anything? (Not likely!)

Start off with a simple question to trigger their thoughts. What in the media or society makes them afraid or scared? Why are they fearful of these things? Are some fears more prevalent or important than others? What fears do their parents or siblings have? Are these fears different than their own? You may get a variety of reactions. Pay attention to your group's answers and allow everyone to express an opinion. You may want to make a list of their suggestions and then pick the three most common fears among themselves or their peers. Then launch into this discussion on fear.

THE DISCUSSION, BY NUMBERS

1. You may want to have your kids check out the answers to these in a dictionary. To be *worried* speaks of negative emotions such as anxiety and fretfulness. To be *concerned* can also mean that, but it has a more positive meaning—to be responsible for or interested in something.

2. How much control do your kids have over these situations? Are they being realistic about their control—or lack of—a situation? You may want to ask for individual responses to these issues. Which ones do they have more control over? Why or why not? Remind them the problems are inevitable, but worrying about them is a choice.

3. Would your kids still worry about these situations? Why or why not? Would they worry if they knew that God has complete control over all problems? And while your kids may question why things happen in their lives, God has his reasons, some of which are beyond our knowing.

4. What does this verse say to your kids? What does a godly person have? How does this affect their beliefs or how they handle situations in their lives?

5. The truths in these verses are powerful—they

give anyone the power to overcome worry. Read and paraphrase each passage with your group. How do your kids feel after reading these verses? How will these verses help them in the future? You may want to have them write down these verses on a 3x5 card for reference when they're feeling the itch to worry.

THE CLOSE

God wants to drive fear from the lives of your kids. Challenge them to be people who trust in God and obey his commands. Encourage your kids to bring their stresses, doubt, and worries to God. He's there with open ears 24 hours a day, seven days a week. And they can be guaranteed that he's listening. Spend some time in prayer with your kids.

Finally, encourage them to seek out a trusted adult to talk with about issues that are really affecting them. Situations of abuse, sexual assault, depression, and family problems may need professional help. For more information, visit the Rape, Abuse, and Incest National Network (www.rainn.org) the National Council on Alcoholism and Drug Dependence, Inc. (http://ncadd.org), Suicide Awareness Voices of Education (www.save.org), the National Foundation For Depressive Illness, Inc. (www.depression.org), or the Youth Specialties Web page (www.YouthSpecialties.com).

MORE

- Worry is a heavy burden. It zaps energy and robs a person of spiritual closeness with God. You may want to read Matthew 11:30, which says "for my yoke is easy, and my burden is light." To illustrate this, gather some large stones or a few other heavy items. Label each of these items with a sin or worry, such as cheating, not getting along with parents, or problems with friends. Then ask for a volunteer to come up and help out. Put all these stones (or other items) into a backpack on the volunteer's back. Point out that sin and worry is like the backpack—an unnecessary burden that they don't have to carry. What removes this burden? Prayer. Point out that praying to God and giving him their worries, doubts, troubles, and sins will remove the burden. Then remove the backpack. God doesn't want Christians to carry around extra weight—he says he'll do it for them. For a fuller explanation of this illustration, see Coming Clean on page 105.
- Encourage your kids to support and encourage each other. You may want to create a weekly prayer list for your group or set up an e-mail list for them to share their prayer requests, worries, and thoughts with each other.

PTL

1. What would you do if you really wanted to **praise** a friend? Put an arrow by all those you would choose to do.

Ignore him or her

Openly admire him or her

Flatter him or her

Criticize him or her

Honor him or her

Express approval of him or her

Cherish him or her

Regard him or her highly

Serve him or her

Respect him or her

Uplift him or her

Tell others about him or her

Other—

2. Check out **Psalm 113.** How does it answer the following questions?

   • Who should be praising the Lord?

   • What are some reasons to praise the Lord?

   • Where should the Lord be praised?

   • When should the Lord be praised?

3. Complete these thoughts with your own ideas. Christians praise God because—

   They can show their praise by—

4. Check your favorite answer in each column below. Why do you praise God?

What God has done for me—
- ❑ saved me
- ❑ died for me
- ❑ provided for me
- ❑ forgiven me
- ❑ listened to me

What God is doing around the world—
- ❑ maintaining creation
- ❑ building the church
- ❑ working miracles
- ❑ answering prayers
- ❑ saving my friends

What I admire about God—
- ❑ his love
- ❑ his justice
- ❑ his greatness
- ❑ his creativity
- ❑ his eternity

5. What **five things** in your life can you praise God for?

PTL [praising God—Psalm 113]

THIS WEEK

God is to be praised! Some teenagers don't understand the importance of praising God and giving him thanks for what he has done for them. Maybe they don't know how to praise him or they're afraid of expressing their feelings to God. This TalkSheet lets your students take a look at praising God and its benefits to believers.

OPENER

One reason people praise God is because he is so much greater than we are. People are nothing compared to God because of his awesomeness. Just look at the world around you. Ask your kids what they think is the most incredible thing they've seen in the world, possibly something in nature, an experience they had, or something else. You may want to make a list of these items. Point out that if God created and allowed these things to be so amazing, he must be unbelievably powerful and mighty! Have your kids thought about that before? Why or why not? How has the world undermined the power of God?

Or present these scenarios: how would you or your kids feel if—

• You've never heard any praises from a coach or teammates, even though you're one of the most valuable players on the team?
• You went out of your way for a friend and never heard a word of thanks?
• You and your lab partner got an A on a science project, but your lab partner got all the credit?
• You babysat four kids for eight hours, but the parents didn't pay you?
• You help out around the house and drive your little brother around, but you never hear a word of appreciation from your parents or guardians?

Most likely, your kids would get bummed after a while. Everyone likes to be praised and given credit for their work. And God does, too. He doesn't need to be built up, but how does praise benefit both Christians and God?

THE DISCUSSION, BY NUMBERS

1. How would your kids praise a friend? Which of these are the best ways to build a friend up? And why is praise important for a friendship or relationship?

2. What does this verse say about praising God? Ask for a few to share their answers. Point out that all believers (the "servants" in the psalm) are to be involved in praising God.

3. How would your kids praise God? What do they think praising him means? What have they learned about praising God from church? Youth group? The Bible?

4. Which answers did you kids choose? You may want to make a poll of the most popular answers and ask them why they chose those items. Then ask your students to give additional examples of the things they most appreciate about God.

5. What five things can each of your kids praise God for? You may want to write all of the items down on a poster board or white board. How would they express their praise for God through prayer? Remind your kids that prayer is simply a one-on-one conversation with God—he's always listening. You may want to write out a prayer of praise as a group.

THE CLOSE

Like friends who need to be praised, God loves to be praised and admired for his awesomeness and blessings. What struggles do your kids have when praising God? Maybe they don't know what to say or how to praise him. Remind your group that they can praise him through their words, their actions, through prayer, and though singing. In fact, they are praising God with their lives. Are their lifestyles showing praise to God? You might want to close by singing a few songs of praise with your group.

MORE

● Encourage your kids to keep a praise list or a journal of the blessings that God has given them. It's easy to forget all the things that God has done for them. You may want to have them add to the list they started in item 5. Encourage them to keep adding to this list throughout the next week and month—and to reflect on this list when praying.

● Your group may be in different places in their relationship with Christ. Others carry huge burdens that are hard to lay aside when giving God praise. Take some time to talk about difficulties and how people can praise God for hard times too. You may want to check out some passages from Romans—the chapter about the life of Paul. He faced all kinds of hardship, yet continued to praise God every day. Read some of these verses with your group, or split your kids up into smaller groups to read a few of these stories. How do Paul's hardships compare to the hardships in the lives of your kids? How can they follow Paul's example of praising God?

IDLE IDOLS

1. Which three items below do you think are the **most important** to teenagers?
   - ❑ Making money
   - ❑ Having a good reputation
   - ❑ Being popular
   - ❑ Being a Christian
   - ❑ Getting good grades
   - ❑ Wearing the right clothes
   - ❑ Making new friends
   - ❑ Being attractive
   - ❑ Having a solid family
   - ❑ Developing talents
   - ❑ Living healthily
   - ❑ Having a girlfriend or a boyfriend
   - ❑ Driving a hot car
   - ❑ Partying
   - ❑ Being in love
   - ❑ Other—

2. How do you know when something is a **high priority**? Check the actions below that apply to each of the three items you chose from the list above.
   - ❑ Commit lots of time to it.
   - ❑ Think or dream about it.
   - ❑ Consume yourself with it.
   - ❑ Work hard to get it or keep it.
   - ❑ Sacrifice other things for it.
   - ❑ Tell others about it.

3. Check out **Psalm 115:2-8** and finish the statement.
   In this psalm, people who worship idols strike me as being—

   Is the world today any different?

4. Now check out **Matthew 6:21**. What would the treasure in your life be?

5. What can you learn about priorities and worship from **Exodus 20:3-4** and **Matthew 22:37**? Which parts of these verses stand out to you the most and why?

IDLE IDOLS [putting God first—Psalm 115]

THIS WEEK

The real teen idols aren't musicians or actors. They're anything that tends to shove God out of the picture. Jesus said, "For where your treasure is, there your heart will be also" (Matthew 6:21). His words explain the problem of idol worship—people's hearts belong to whatever they value the most! This TalkSheet will challenge your students to examine their priorities in light of the psalmist's comparison of the living God and dead idols.

OPENER

There are all kinds of distractions in the lives of your kids. Start off by asking your kids to write out the schedule for a typical day in their life. Ask them to be precise—to write down exactly what they normally do at a given time. Then have your kids share a few of their schedules. What consumes most of their time during a day? Between your kids, tally up how many hours they spend sleeping, watching TV, studying, playing sports, or eating. You might be surprised at the results.

Then ask which of these in their lives take priority. On a scale of 1 to 5 (1 being the most important), how would they rate the priorities in their lives? Then ask them how God fits into this schedule. How many minutes are spent praying to him, reading the Bible, or just hanging out with God? Most likely, it's not very much time compared to all the other activities. If they were to schedule time for God, where would they put it? Then let your kids know that time—and all the activities in their lives—can become idols. Idols are anything that pulls their attention away from God. This includes people, activities, or events.

THE DISCUSSION, BY NUMBERS

1. What did your kids put in the middle of the target? What other two priorities do kids their age have in their lives? Take a tally of these and then ask why these are such big priorities. Do any of your kids have spending time with God as a priority? Why or why not?

2. Teenagers have all kinds of idols in their lives today. How do these priorities rate in their lives? Why are some emphasized as being so important? How has culture influenced this?

3. You may get a lot of different answers for this one. Point out the foolishness of valuing things over God. Verse 8 is helpful—the implication is that people who place their trust in things will eventually wind up spiritually dead, unfeeling, and blind.

4. How did your kids paraphrase this verse? Ask for a few to share their paraphrases. Communicate to the group that anything that takes priority over God takes a person's heart away from God. Let them discuss the priorities from question 1, debating whether these things are a real danger to the average person's relationship with God.

5. What insights or lessons did they pull out of these verses? How can they realistically apply these verses to their lives today? What can they change to start focusing more on God and less on other things?

THE CLOSE

God can do mighty things for people who put him first in their lives. But this isn't easy for any Christian, teenagers included. Take some time to discuss things putting God first in their lives. Do they give God control of every day? Do they hand over their problems and concerns to him? Do they glorify him with their friendships, schoolwork, or use of money? Challenge your kids to take small steps toward God and get into the habit of putting him first. And start by closing in prayer with your kids, giving them time to take a look at themselves and their relationships with God.

MORE

● Ask your kids if they know any Christians who put God before everything else. Do they know any celebrities or sports figures who openly share their faith about God? What about a classmate, parent, or sibling? Encourage them to share their stories or examples. How do these people set an example for your kids through their actions and beliefs? You may want to share a story of your own, or find a story about someone who you respect and admire.

● One way to put God first is to get to know him better. Encourage your kids to learn more about God and get to know him better as a friend. How many of your kids have read the Bible? Or started journaling their thoughts about God or prayer? Challenge your group to take tangible steps to getting closer to God. You may want to start a small group study on God. For information or resources for you and your teens, check out www.YouthSpecialties.com.

SOUL POLLUTION

1. List **four things** that you think pollute the minds and souls of teenagers.

2. Who do you think should decide what is **soul pollution** for you?

   - ❏ Parents
   - ❏ Yourself
   - ❏ Your school
   - ❏ The government
   - ❏ Teachers
   - ❏ The media
   - ❏ Church leaders
   - ❏ Friends
   - ❏ God
   - ❏ Other—

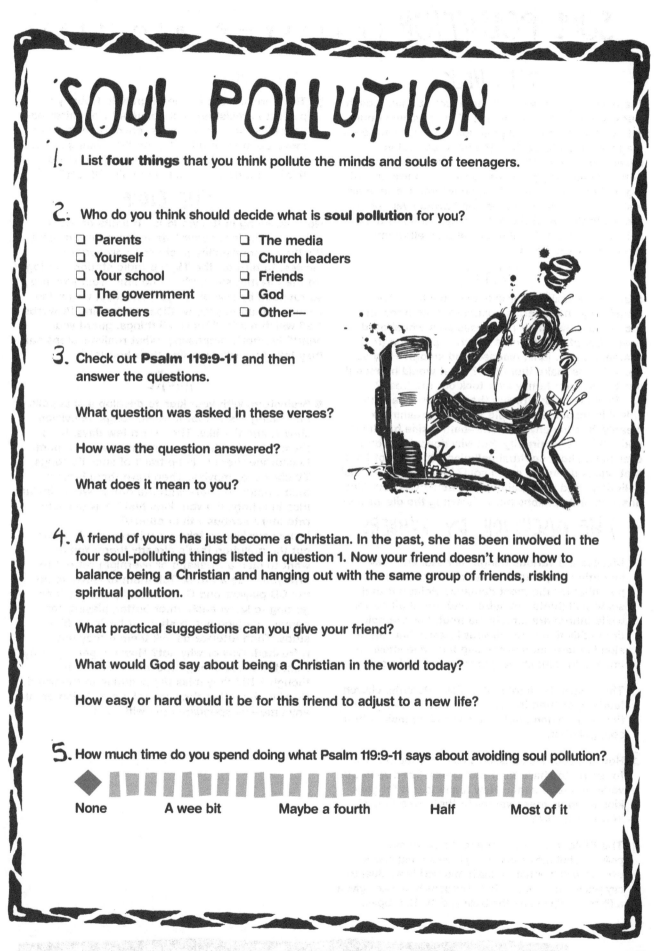

3. Check out **Psalm 119:9-11** and then answer the questions.

   What question was asked in these verses?

   How was the question answered?

   What does it mean to you?

4. A friend of yours has just become a Christian. In the past, she has been involved in the four soul-polluting things listed in question 1. Now your friend doesn't know how to balance being a Christian and hanging out with the same group of friends, risking spiritual pollution.

   What practical suggestions can you give your friend?

   What would God say about being a Christian in the world today?

   How easy or hard would it be for this friend to adjust to a new life?

5. How much time do you spend doing what Psalm 119:9-11 says about avoiding soul pollution?

   ◆ ▮▮▮▮▮▮▮▮▮▮▮▮▮▮▮▮▮▮▮▮▮▮▮▮▮▮ ◆

   None   A wee bit   Maybe a fourth   Half   Most of it

SOUL POLLUTION [purity — Psalm 119]

THIS WEEK

Teens who spend two or three hours at church each week are bombarded the rest of their waking hours with pollution—spiritual pollution. It's everywhere—in magazines, on television, the Internet, and in movies. In Psalm 119:9-11, David asked how a young person could stay pure. The answer? To live according to God's word, seek him, obey him, and take his instructions to heart. Teens can't avoid everything the world throws at them, but they can learn to be selective and careful about what they allow into their minds and hearts.

OPENER

Start off by asking your kids this question—how would they characterize pollution? Take a few minutes to jot down their responses on a whiteboard or poster board. What words describe pollution (for example, trash, junk, disease, and smog)? How do these things make them feel? What would happen if not one in their family ever took out the trash?

Pollution is destroying the earth and wasting valuable resources. People make maintaining a cleanly, healthy environment—both inside buildings and outdoors—a priority. But why doesn't anyone ever think about spiritual pollution—the kind of junk that builds up inside one's soul? What exactly is soul pollution? And what pollutes the soul? Get your kids' answers and opinions before starting the discussion.

THE DISCUSSION, BY NUMBERS

1. Discuss the various things your students have identified as pollutants. Which items have the potential for the most damage? Point out that some pollutants are subtle and not at all obvious, while others are directly harmful. For example, drug addiction is an obvious hazard, but television is more subtle—robbing time and showing images that numb people to wrong and right.

2. The answer is simple—the Bible. Parents, church leaders, or friends can have a role in giving direction and wisdom, but God gives clear insight into soul pollution.

3. How did your kids answer these questions? Ask for some to share their responses. Then read the verse out loud again. How realistic is it for your kids to apply these verses to their lives today? Why or why not?

4. The Bible gives wisdom about how to avoid pollution, but the responsibility is yours. You decide what to watch or not to watch. You decide whether to say yes to drugs or not. But Christians have been given a filter to help them—the Bible and the Holy Spirit.

5. The Christian life is one of growth. Nobody is perfect in resisting soul pollution! No matter how your kids rated themselves, encourage them to move up at least one step on their rating scale. What are some tangible ways for them to do this? What do the verses in Psalm 119 say?

THE CLOSE

Not everything in the world is off limits or avoidable—the key is for your kids to learn discernment. It's their responsibility to choose appropriate movies, to turn off the TV, flip radio stations, or log off the Internet sites. It's a fine line—your kids are surrounded by sexual images, violence, vulgar language, and pornography. Close by reading Proverbs 4:23 which reads, "Above all things, guard your heart" (author's emphasis). What realistic steps can they take towards guarding their hearts?

MORE

● Brainstorm with your kids to develop a soul pollution rating system for movies, songs, television shows, and the like. Then for a few days, have them rate what they see and hear around them. Encourage them to keep track of specific songs, TV shows, or movies. Then have them bring in their ratings to share with the group. What similarities in ratings did your kids find? Why did some rate more seriously than others?

● Invite your kids to take a soul shower—to clean out the pollution that's already there. You may want to plan a weekend or overnight retreat to give your kids a break. Tell them to leave home the CD players and Gameboys. Spend the time getting to know each other better, playing some games, hanging out, resting, or having a Bible study. Then afterwards ask them if they felt refreshed. Why or why not? How did getting away from the world change the way they felt or thought? Did they miss the pollution of the world? Remind them that they can take a pollution break any time—by spending time with God.

ASKING WHY

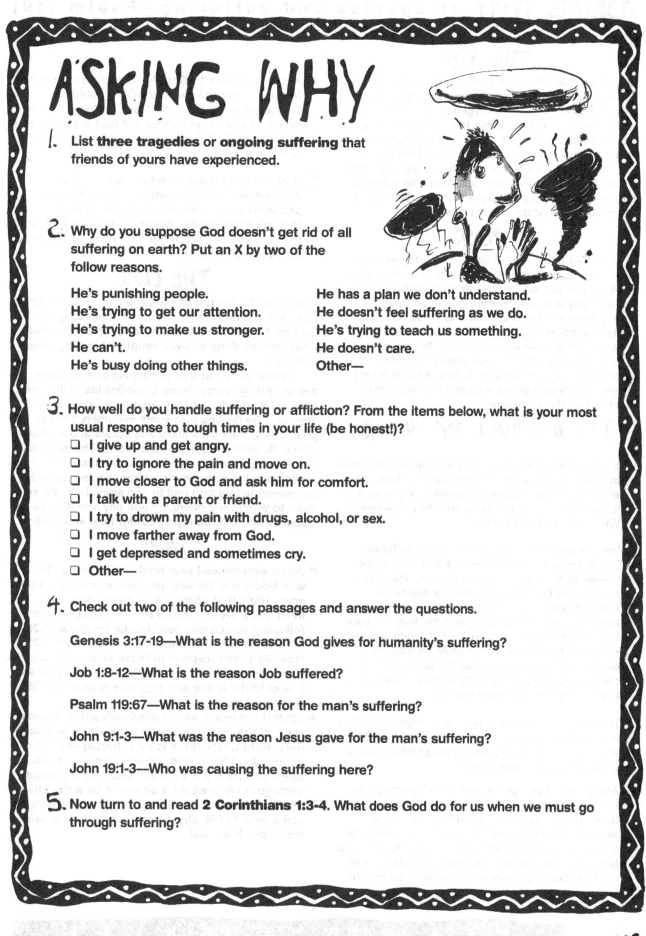

1. List **three tragedies** or **ongoing suffering** that friends of yours have experienced.

2. Why do you suppose God doesn't get rid of all suffering on earth? Put an X by two of the follow reasons.

He's punishing people.
He's trying to get our attention.
He's trying to make us stronger.
He can't.
He's busy doing other things.

He has a plan we don't understand.
He doesn't feel suffering as we do.
He's trying to teach us something.
He doesn't care.
Other—

3. How well do you handle suffering or affliction? From the items below, what is your most usual response to tough times in your life (be honest!)?
   ❑ I give up and get angry.
   ❑ I try to ignore the pain and move on.
   ❑ I move closer to God and ask him for comfort.
   ❑ I talk with a parent or friend.
   ❑ I try to drown my pain with drugs, alcohol, or sex.
   ❑ I move farther away from God.
   ❑ I get depressed and sometimes cry.
   ❑ Other—

4. Check out two of the following passages and answer the questions.

   Genesis 3:17-19—What is the reason God gives for humanity's suffering?

   Job 1:8-12—What is the reason Job suffered?

   Psalm 119:67—What is the reason for the man's suffering?

   John 9:1-3—What was the reason Jesus gave for the man's suffering?

   John 19:1-3—Who was causing the suffering here?

5. Now turn to and read **2 Corinthians 1:3-4**. What does God do for us when we must go through suffering?

ASKING WHY [tragedies and suffering—Psalm 119]

THIS WEEK

Why does God allow suffering? That's a tough question—especially when he allows it to happen to us. This TalkSheet discusses tragedies and suffering—and points out that the Bible has some answers and provides lots of comfort. Keep in mind that some of your students may be experiencing suffering that you don't know about. Be sensitive to your students' responses throughout this TalkSheet and follow up with encouragement to speak with an adult about any problems that they may be facing.

OPENER

To start things off, you may want to bring in some newspaper or magazine articles (or articles printed from a news source on the Internet) that describe various tragedies and suffering. Maybe there has been a recent local event that captured your students' attention. Ask for their responses. Which ones are more severe than others? Is one more painful than the others? How would your kids respond to these situations, if they were in them? Finally, how would being a Christian affect their reactions to the situations?

THE DISCUSSION, BY NUMBERS

1. Everyone experiences pain and trials in their lives in some degree—even in high school. Allow your students to express any tragedies they have personally faced and the emotions they experienced. What about their friends?

2. Your students may know that some suffering is the direct result of human action, but some seems to be beyond human control. This item focuses on God's part of the equation—the things beyond their control (some illnesses, injuries, natural disasters, and the like). As your kids discuss each item on the list, point out the suffering that Jesus faced while he was on earth—ridicule, hatred, physical pain, and even death (see More for specific verses to use for discussing this with your group).

3. How do your kids react to pain in their lives? You may want to take a poll of your group. Why do some react differently than others? Which reactions are worse than others?

4. Assign one passage to each small group (or to individuals) and ask the group to discuss each item. They may come up with the following answers. (1) Adam and Eve and all of humanity suffer because of disobedience. (2) Job suffered because Satan was permitted to challenge him. (3) The author of Psalm 119 suffered so that he would turn back to God. (4) The blind man suffered in order that he and others could see God's power at work. (5) Jesus suffered at the hands of evil people. Point out that suffering can come from God, from ourselves, from others, and from Satan.

5. God comforts those who turn to him. But that does not mean that he immediately takes our problems away. It means he helps us walk through our troubles. Ask your students how God may be able to help in the situations they discussed in question 1.

THE CLOSE

Whatever the source of the problems in the lives of your group members? Encourage them to go to God for his comfort. He's there for them, no matter what they've done or what relationship they have with him.

Finally, point out that some pain and suffering doesn't just go away. Some tragedies last a lifetime. Some of your kids—or their friends or family member—may be dealing with some extremely serious problems in their lives (including sexual abuse, drug abuse, depression, suicide, and more). These situations need professional help—your kids must find a trusted adult (pastor, youth worker, teacher, school counselor) to talk with and to find some help. Be sensitive to your group members and pay attention to students who may be crying out for help and healing.

MORE

- Jesus experienced pain firsthand. Although he was God's son, he was also human and faced the same trials that people face today—and more, including a brutal, painful death. Check out the following verses with your group: Matthew 27:28-50, Matthew 4:1-10, Mark 14:65, and 1 Peter 2:23. How did Christ respond to these situations? Do your kids think he felt pain? And how can your kids model Christ in the way that they respond to difficulties in their lives?

- What if the world wasn't filled with pain? You may want to ask your students to brainstorm an imaginary world where there is no suffering—but where people don't know God. What would be the advantages of such a place? What would be the disadvantages? What would it be like to be a Christian and feel no pain? Finally, you may want to take some time to talk about heaven and what a painless place it will be!

WASTING TIME

1. Define **potential** in your own words.

2. Check out **Psalm 127** and then answer the following items.

   a. Verse 1 talks about a house and a city, which represent a family and a community of people. What do you think this verse is saying about families and communities that make God a priority?

   b. Verse 2 speaks of toiling in vain without God. What do you think this verse is saying about finding purpose in work?

   c. Verses 3 to 5 center on the value of children to a family. What lessons do we learn about kids in each of the three verses?

3. How much do you think a person's meaning in life goes up when God is involved? Rate your response with an X on the scale below.

| God can make a person's life worse. | No difference—people don't need God for meaning. | God adds meaning only for those who become missionaries or pastors. | Without God there is no real meaning in life. |

4. How **meaningful** so you think your life is? Check one or more of the following statements that best describes your thoughts.
   - ❑ I think my life is meaningless and boring.
   - ❑ I believe there's no such thing as meaning.
   - ❑ I'm trying to find meaning.
   - ❑ I have a lot of potential, but for what?
   - ❑ I think the closer I get to God, the more my life counts.
   - ❑ I will never have a great life.
   - ❑ I know God can give my life meaning.
   - ❑ I strive to be the best I can be in life.
   - ❑ I expect my life to have meaning once I'm on my own.
   - ❑ I trust God to help me have meaning in life.

5. You're written an e-mail to God asking him to help you live up to your true potential and lead a meaningful life. What do you think God would write back?

WASTING TIME [your purpose in life—Psalm 127]

THIS WEEK

Your students are essentially young lives under construction, like the house mentioned in Psalm 127:1. Each student's "building" will stand the test of time only if it is set on the foundation of God and built by Jesus the carpenter. This TalkSheet discusses the need to wisely construct lives according to the will of God.

OPENER

Write this statement on a whiteboard or poster board—THE BEST WAY TO MAKE MY LIFE COUNT WOULD BE TO_____. Let your kids suggest answers or have them write answers on slips of paper that you collect and read. You may want to write down their responses or have them share them as a group. What do they think about the potential of their lives? How do they think they can make a difference in the world? Then let them know that the topic of discussion is finding meaning and purpose in life.

THE DISCUSSION, BY NUMBERS

1. Potential is something that can develop or become actual. In life, it's realizing significance and purpose. Point out that while everything has potential of some kind, potential takes effort to be realized.

2. God claims that he is the one who gives meaning and purpose to life. Encourage your students not to make the mistake of excluding God from their lives. He's given them each unique gifts and talents to use for his glory. And he'll bless your kids and use their gifts for his will if they're willing to let him!

3. Some students may feel that a life is meaningful in godly terms only if a person is in full-time Christian service. Point out that everyone—including young people in high school—can lead lives of genuine purpose and significance when they live for God.

4. How meaningful do your kids think their lives are? You may want to ask for some to respond. Encourage everyone to realize that faith is required to see the importance of our lives. Remind them of Gideon, who was a weak man when the angel of the Lord called him a mighty warrior (Judges 6:12). He wasn't a warrior yet, but he soon would be. In the same way, your kids can be assured that, while they may not see themselves as important in God's plans now, they'll be able to look back at their meaningful lives someday—if they stick close to the Lord.

5. How do your kids think God would respond? Ask for a few of them to share their e-mail responses. Then discuss ways your kids can grow close to God—commitment to prayer, Bible reading, fellowship with other believers, and so on.

THE CLOSE

What would your kids like to hear said about them if their accomplishments were called out as they entered heaven (sort of a reverse obituary)? You may want to have them make a list of items for themselves. Are those accomplishments possible in their lives? Why or why not? Then ask them to describe how God fits into all the things suggested. What difference can he make in their lives?

MORE

- Do your kids know what their spiritual gifts are? You may want to do a spiritual gifts inventory with your kids. It's an excellent way for your kids to learn more about themselves and what gifts God has given them. For more information on resources or to order, check out Youth Specialties (www.YouthSpecialties.com), Zondervan Publishing House (www.zondervan.com), Christianbook.com (www.christianbooks.com), or Gospel Light (www.GospelLight.com).

- Or ask your church staff to help you gather the names of older men and women in the congregation who have led rich, meaningful lives for God. Ask your group to write some of these people, asking them to share the ways God has given their lives meaning and purpose. You should include a cover letter explaining the reason for the request. Then share their responses with the group. How has God worked in their lives?

UNITY

1. Think of a situation when you were part of a team (or partnership) that accomplished a goal. How did you feel being part of this team?

2. Take a look at **Psalm 133:1** and **Ephesians 4:9-12**. Then sum up the main idea of these passages in two sentences.

3. Below are some words and phrases that describe Christian friendship and some of its advantages. Circle **five** that you think apply to your life—and to teamwork—the most.

Trust	Uniformity	Friendship
Unity	Same goals	Competition
Teamwork	Honesty	Sincerity
Togetherness	Clique	Partnership
Loyalty	Encouragement	
Independence	Hard work	

4. How could friends work together in unity to help in the following situations?

   a. A classmate at school asks you to answer some tough questions about God.

   b. The new girl (or guy) in school is struggling to make friends (and is being made fun of).

   c. Someone close to you has an illness, and it might be fatal.

5. The people you're with in your youth group are a team. Check one item to describe what you think.
   - ❑ Our group really is a team. We work together well.
   - ❑ I feel that I'm an important part of this team.
   - ❑ Our team would be willing to do something important.
   - ❑ Our group is growing as a team.
   - ❑ I don't feel part of a team at all.
   - ❑ Our group is definitely *not* a team.
   - ❑ A team? What's that?

UNITY [Christian friendship—Psalm 133]

THIS WEEK

What is Christian friendship? Essentially, it can be defined as friendship with unity and purpose. Your teens know what friendship is, but do they know that they're part of a unified group? And that this group is strong and can accomplish a great deal of good? This TalkSheet deals with things that united Christian teens can do that will make an impact in the lives of others.

OPENER

The last part of Ecclesiastes 4:12 says, "A cord of three strands is not quickly broken." Read this sentence to your students or write it on a whiteboard. What important lesson or lessons do they think it teaches? What does this verse say about friendship and teamwork? You may want to demonstrate this verse by challenging a few volunteers to break a thread wrapped around their two fingers. It's easy if the thread is wrapped around once, but difficult if wrapped around several times!

THE DISCUSSION, BY NUMBERS

1. Encourage your students to describe in detail what the teamwork experience was like, including feelings, successes, frustrations, and so on. Could your kids have accomplished the goal alone as easily—or at all? How does being part of a team make a person stronger?

2. Point out that the term *brothers* in Psalm 133 is synonymous with friends and family. The advantages of teamwork—summed up—are that people working together accomplish more and can help each other when the going gets tough. Why do your kids think God is a fan of teamwork?

3. Which words did your kids choose to describe teamwork in their lives? In the situations described in question 1, which of these elements were part of their experiences? Which of these items are necessary for effective teamwork? Why or why not? As a group, choose the top 10 items that are needed for teamwork in your youth group. You may want to post this list for your group to see later on.

4. How would your kids handle these situations? How would teamwork or unity help these situations? What difference would it make in the life of the person described? How can teamwork strengthen a person's relationship with God?

5. Your students may think of your group as anything from totally splintered to tight-knit. You may want to ask your kids for their ratings on these items and keep a consensus on a whiteboard. Or collect the TalkSheets to get their answers. How does the group rate itself? What has made it strong or has weakened it? And what steps can your kids take to make your group stronger? Brainstorm areas of need that your student team could work to fulfill. You may want to plan an activity or event that you could do as a group to build teamwork.

THE CLOSE

Teamwork is an important aspect of Christian friendship. In a sense, Christians are part of a big family that works together for the glory of God. Relationships of any kind—friendship, families, teams, youth groups—take work! Challenge your kids to start working on their relationships with Christians around them. You may want to plan a weekend retreat or activity to build the relationships within your group. For retreat or event ideas, check out www.YouthSpecialties.com for resources, including *Student Underground, Ideas Library: Camps, Missions,* and *Service Ideas for Youth Groups,* and more.

MORE

● As a group, make a list of goals that your group would like to accomplish within the next few months or school year. This may include an event or activity that they would like to plan or sponsor. Then organize the team into smaller groups and assign responsibilities for various aspects of reaching the goal, including a prayer group, a planning group, a publicity group, etc. Keep track of the effectiveness of your team as it seeks to reach whatever goal or goals it has selected. Afterward you may want to debrief your group on the success of the event and how teamwork played a role in it.

● Part of being a team is knowing what to contribute to the group. Everyone has different gifts or strengths to contribute to a team. If you haven't already gone through a spiritual gifts inventory (recommended in the previous TalkSheet), you may want to walk though this with your kids. Possibly take a weekend retreat to do this. For more information on resources or to order, check out Youth Specialties (www.YouthSpecialties.com), Zondervan Publishing House (www.zondervan.com), Christianbook.com (www.christianbooks.com), or Gospel Light (www.GospelLight.com).

BETTER THAN YOU

1. Reality check! On the scale below, where would you put yourself?
(Be honest! Your answers are confidential.)

◆ ▮▮▮▮▮▮▮▮▮▮▮▮▮▮▮▮▮▮▮▮ ◆

Everyone is better than me   I'm better than most people

Why did you rate yourself in the way you did?

2. What do you think of conceited people?
In my experience they're usually—

   ❑ no better than others   ❑ glued to the mirror
   ❑ fooling themselves   ❑ well-liked by themselves
   ❑ to be envied   ❑ grudgingly admired
   ❑ in need of deflation   ❑ easy to get to know
   ❑ well-liked by others   ❑ good listeners
   ❑ really nice to losers   ❑ insecure

3. Check out these verses to see what they teach about pride.

   Psalm 138:6   God's attitude toward pride is—
   Proverbs 16:18   The eventual results of pride are—
   Romans 12:3   Prideful people think—
   Galatians 6:3   Prideful people do—

4. How would you answer this statement?
To get an accurate picture of yourself, you should—

   ❑ trust your inner instincts
   ❑ compare yourself to famous people
   ❑ ignore what other people say
   ❑ use a camera
   ❑ pray that God gives you sound judgment
   ❑ realize your worth comes from Christ
   ❑ ask people for their honest criticism
   ❑ read the Bible to see how you measure up to
     God's standards

5. What do you think? When it comes to pride in my life, I think I—

BETTER THAN YOU [conceit—Psalm 138]

THIS WEEK

Teenagers ridicule conceited people, and most would probably deny they suffer from conceit. But it can show itself in many forms, including exclusive cliques, superiority complexes, argumentative attitudes, and—worst of all—lack of interest in God. This TalkSheet will help students discover the dangers of conceit and what to do about it.

OPENER

What other words do your kids think of when they hear the word *conceit*? Some examples may be arrogance, vanity, being stuck-up, pride or snobbery. You may want to make a list of their suggestions for them to see. Now ask them how they respond to a person who shows these characteristics. What emotional responses do they have to conceit? Most likely they'll have negative responses. What do your kids think causes conceit? On a scale of 1 to 10 (1 being "Not a big deal" and 10 being "It's extremely dangerous"), how would your group rate the dangers of pride or conceit? Why did they give these ratings?

THE DISCUSSION, BY NUMBERS

1. Keep this one confidential and don't ask for individual responses. This one gets your kids thinking about how they think about themselves in comparison with others. You may want to ask how many rated themselves over five. Let them know that anything over eight could be hurtful to their relationships with others, themselves, and God. Anyone is in that danger zone, needs to think seriously about the pride factor in his or her life.

2. What were the most common responses from your group? What makes each of these items dangerous in a person's life? As students discuss each point, bring up other problems such as social exclusiveness, selfishness, poor team membership, and disregard for God.

3. Take some time to go over each verse and to discuss the responses from your kids. Point out that the Bible makes it clear that pride is a big problem. It angers God, leads to destruction, and involves poor judgment and self-deception.

4. Romans 12:3 gives a key to curing pride: "Do not think of yourself more highly than you ought, but rather think of yourself with sober judgment." Your kids need to evaluate themselves accurately. Challenge your kids to take a serious look at themselves. How well do they relate to others? How is their relationship with God? Do they often think of themselves first, or are they willing to make sacrifices for others?

5. As a follow-up to item 4, how do your kids feel about pride in their lives? Some may say that pride isn't an issue with them, but others may feel that they need help in this area. Don't ask for individual answers. Instead encourage them to think of ways that they can apply Psalm 138 to their lives.

THE CLOSE

Proverbs 16:18 says "Pride goes before destruction, a haughty spirit before a fall." Pride is sin. But God stands ready to forgive us when we confess our sins. God warns in Proverbs that pride leads to destruction. In other words, conceit is dangerous in the lives of Christians. It ruins friendships, damages relationships, and hinders closeness with God. Close with a time of prayer for your kids to evaluate their pride and to ask God for forgiveness—and for strength to focus on him and not on themselves.

MORE

● How does pride relate to humility? Humble people usually have quite a bit of humility—that is, they're willing to do anything for anyone. They think of themselves last and others first, even if it means being humiliated in what they do or scorned by others. Take a look at the life of Christ. He was the epitome of humility—going so far as to die for those he loves. Check out these passages with your group and discuss the humble nature of Christ. How did he reflect love through his actions? How did others around him react? And how can your kids model Christ's humbleness in their own lives?

● How does one balance pride with self-respect? Some of your kids may struggle with their self-esteem, in which case they either have no pride or too much of it. Take some time to talk about loving oneself versus being proud. Read Luke 10:27 and note that God commands people to love others—as they love themselves. That is, God commands Christians to love and respect themselves—to think highly of themselves and value who they are. Do your kids have healthy self-esteem? Why or why not? How can they love themselves without going overboard?

HE KNOWS YOU

1. What do you think God thinks of abortion, suicide, mercy killing, and murder?

2. Check out **Psalm 139:13-16** and answer the following questions.

   a. In verse 13, what part does God take in a person's birth and life?

   b. In verse 14, how does the author rate God's part in a person's birth and life?

   c. In verses 15 and 16, how carefully was God watching over David's early development?

   d. In verse 16, what clue do we find that God carefully watches over all the days of our lives?

   e. What do these truths tell you about the value that God places on every person?

3. Read **Romans 5:8**. What price did Jesus pay in order to save our lives? And what does this tell you about the value God places on every person?

4. What do you think—**Y** (yes), **N** (no), or **M** (maybe)?
   ___ People don't listen to Christians when they talk about human life.
   ___ Society is moving toward a greater respect for life.
   ___ The more educated a person is, the more respect he has for life.
   ___ I can't do anything to help give value to human life.

5. List ways you can show respect for human life in the following situations.
   I could help a disabled person by—
   I could help a person get closer to God by—
   I could stand up for this important truth by—

HE KNOWS YOU [the sanctity of life—Psalm 139]

THIS WEEK

The value of life in today's society seems so cheap—abortion, assisted suicide, and murder are just a few examples of the way our world has disregarded the life God gives. God places a supreme value on each life, and that value is the suffering and death of Jesus Christ. God's plan for each valuable life starts long before conception, and his plan is good. Use this TalkSheet to discuss the Christian responsibility to uphold respect for the life God has given each person.

OPENER

Start off by writing the words SANCTITY OF LIFE on the whiteboard or poster board. Ask your students to define what they think the phrase means. What examples from television, movies, government policies, school, and so on do they have that reflect either positive or negative views of the sanctity of life? What news stories have they heard lately that have dealt with this issue? You may want to bring in a newspaper or magazine with a few examples. In what ways are lives abused by people today? What is the cause of the destruction of life today? What does this say about human power and control?

THE DISCUSSION, BY NUMBERS

1. What were the responses that your kids gave? You may get some emotional reactions as your students get involved in the discussion. Your group most likely will reach a consensus and that's okay. But do make sure they understand the main point of this exercise—God does have an outlook on the sanctity of human life, and Christians should uphold it as best as we're able to understand it.

2. What does this passage have to say about God's involvement in birth and life? Point out that God's involvement shows that he considers each of us to be valuable.

3. The fact that Christ died for all people (1 John 2:2) shows that the Lord values us more than we could ever imagine. Humans can't start to fathom God's love for his children. In light of this verse alone, how does God feel about harming his creation and the lives he's given us?

4. How did your kids respond to these statements? You may want to take a poll of your group to get their responses. Point out that God has put humans in charge of taking care of life on earth—and has given Christians greater responsibilities to care for and respect life.

5. Your kids may have different responses to these. Challenge them to think realistically about these. Encourage them to think of specific, small ways that they can show respect for life. The first of these is simply showing respect for God's creation and the value that he's given every person.

THE CLOSE

How should Christians react to others who seem to disregard the sanctity of life? What tangible, realistic ways can your kids help raise the value of life at their schools, workplaces, or church? Some of your kids may have dealt with or faced suicide or abortion. Be sensitive to your students' responses throughout this TalkSheet. Finally, remind your group that God forgives sins—including abusing or disregarding life.

MORE

● You may want to have your kids (or groups of them) do some research about the sanctity of life in America (or a different country, if you want to add some variety). Encourage them to find statistics on abortion, murder, hate crimes, and the like that can be drawn from news magazines and Web sites. See if they can find differences between states—for example, some states allow abortions to minors without parental consent. Talk about their findings at the next meeting. What do these reports say about the sanctity of life? Has it improved over the years or not?

● Challenge your kids to a debate! Split up your group in half and assign each side a stand on a certain issue. You may want to provide your group with a copy of the Bill of Rights (found online at http://lcweb2.loc.gov/const/bor.html), a Bible, and maybe some statistics. Each group must defend its stand by backing up its arguments with these resources. Then let the two sides go at it.

Encourage them to them to think the issues through from both sides. Assign one chief speaker from each group to control who speaks and when. You may want to have a four-seat forum—four chairs in the middle of the group, two seats for each side. Only those in the chairs can argue and anyone who wants to speak must replace a person in a chair. Some issues include pro-abortion versus anti-abortion, death penalty versus no death penalty, euthanasia versus no euthanasia, and freedom for hate groups versus limited freedoms.

DIVINE DESERT

1. How would you finish this statement?
When I feel distant from God, it's usually because—

2. Check out **Psalm 143**. How was the author (David) feeling as he wrote it? Why?

3. Which response below would you choose to finish this statement?
A Christian who is feeling down spiritually—
   ❑ is probably committing a sin that causes guilt.
   ❑ should read the Bible, pray, and go to church more.
   ❑ can be a solid, committed Christian without major sins.
   ❑ needs to get some extra sleep.

4. Here's a list of things that might help a person get back on track with spirituality. Which **two** would be the most helpful for you and why?
   ❑ Moving to a new place to start over
   ❑ Making new friends
   ❑ Volunteering or doing good deeds
   ❑ Going to a Bible study
   ❑ Breaking some habits, such as drugs or alcohol abuse
   ❑ Spending more time with God
   ❑ Going to a Christian school
   ❑ Taking a break from going to church
   ❑ Other—

5. Now read **John 13:14-17**. What lesson was Jesus trying to teach his followers?

What result did he promise to those who lived according to this lesson?

From *High School TalkSheets Psalms and Proverbs—Updated!* by Rick Bundschuh and Tom Finley. Permission to reproduce this page granted only for use in the buyer's own youth group. www.YouthSpecialties.com

59

DIVINE DESERT [spiritual dry spells—Psalm 143]

THIS WEEK

All Christians have ups and downs in their relationship with God. But this isn't a sign that God has abandoned them. God doesn't move! It's people that move away from God in different ways. This TalkSheet discusses emotional and spiritual ups and downs—and how to deal with those as Christians.

OPENER

Start off by asking your kids to make a map or chart of their relationship with God. Provide paper and pens for them to do this. Let them create their own chart—pinpointing specific times when they felt up or down in their relationship with God. Ask them to write down what times those were and what was going on in their lives at the time. Be sure to have them mark the beginning of their relationship with God and where they are today. They won't have to share these maps or charts with anyone else, so encourage them to be honest about the challenges they've faced. Afterwards, ask the group to summarize what causes someone to lose touch with God. Why do they think people go through highs and lows? How do they think God responds when he sees them going through really good times and rough times, too?

THE DISCUSSION, BY NUMBERS

1. Without forcing your kids to share their individual answers, ask them to make a list of the things that tend to make them feel distant from God. You may want to hang a large sheet of white paper for them to write their answers on. Make it clear that there's a big difference between feeling that God is far off and him really being far off.

2. In these verses David felt hopeless and depressed. He felt faint and dismayed. His trials were severe (verse 3) and it had been a long time since he felt good (verses 5 and 6). And it seems that he hadn't gotten any answers to his prayers (verse 7). But despite all this, he didn't feel that God was far away. He still turned to God in prayer, recognizing that God was near.

3. How did your kids respond to these items? Ask them to explain why they answered yes or no. Then relate these items to David in Psalm 143. Was he committing a sin or not praying? Was he committed to God?

4. So when the down times come, how will your kids respond? What answers did they choose from these items? Ask for a few volunteers to share their responses and why they chose the ones they did. Take a poll among your group members

to see how they answered. How easy or difficult is it to follow through with these suggestions? Why or why not?

5. What did Jesus say to his followers in these verses? If your group had to paraphrase the verses in their own words, what would they say? How do these verses apply directly to the lives of your kids today?

THE CLOSE

Your kids have control over their emotions—and over how they respond to the down times in Christianity. To illustrate this, ask your kids to describe the possible emotional responses a girl might have to being asked out by a guy. She could be happy (if she liked him), mad (if he was going steady with someone else), disgusted (if he was a creep), and so forth. The emotional response is up to her. The same thing applies to down times with God. If you're going through a hard time, how will your kids respond to God? Will they walk away? Or will they lean harder on him? The choice is up to them. God never moves.

MORE

● Have your kids take a look at the charts or maps from the introduction. Looking at the down times, how could they have handled these situations differently? What would have made a difference at the time? During these times, did they move toward God or away from him? Would it have helped to talk with someone, like a youth pastor or teacher? Were their prayers answered? If so, how? Did God prove himself to be faithful through these times? If your students are comfortable with each other, you may want to let them share a few struggles—and the results—with each other.

● Maybe you have some group members who need some encouragement in their relationship with God. You may want to form a small prayer group or a daily e-mail verse and encouragement. Or make a goal to have lunch with one student every week to see how they're doing in their walk with God. Some of your kids may be dealing with some pretty heavy issues, such as depression, abuse, social struggles, problems at home and more. They may be asking the question why? and may need to find professional help or someone to help them deal with these issues.

SMART LIVING

1. **Which of the following people would you go to for advice about a problem?**
   - ❏ A successful songwriter
   - ❏ A college professor
   - ❏ A football star
   - ❏ A bag lady
   - ❏ A teacher
   - ❏ A youth pastor
   - ❏ An Internet chat room acquaintance
   - ❏ A friend your own age
   - ❏ An older brother or sister
   - ❏ A parent or adult relative
   - ❏ A complete stranger
   - ❏ A counselor
   - ❏ A boyfriend or girlfriend
   - ❏ A psychic hotline
   - ❏ A police officer
   - ❏ A writer of an advice column
   - ❏ A book called *Smart Answers for Dummies*
   - ❏ Other—

2. **Now go back to the list above and circle the top three that you have the highest degree of respect for. What makes you respect or admire these sources?**

3. **Suppose you were about to be ushered into the presence of God himself. What words would you choose to describe what you might feel?**

4. **Check out Proverbs 1:7. In your own words what do you think this passage means?**

5. **What do you think a person's behavior would be like if he or she took Proverbs 1:7 seriously? Why?**

6. **Place an X on the line to show the degree of fearful respect you have towards God.**

◆ ▮▮▮▮▮▮▮▮▮▮▮▮▮▮▮▮▮▮▮▮ ◆

Zero   **A Ton**

SMART LIVING [respecting God — Proverbs 1]

THIS WEEK

"The fear of the Lord is the beginning of knowledge, but fools despise wisdom and discipline" (Proverbs 1:7). Teenagers seek wisdom and advice from many foolish sources—movies, cultural trends, horoscopes, fashion magazines, and more. This TalkSheet is designed to help students understand the relationship between wise choices and having a fear of God.

OPENER

Start off this discussion by asking your students if they've ever received an electrical shock. What was the experience like? How did they get the shock? Did they stick their fingers in a socket? Rub their stocking feet on the carpet and then touch someone else? Were they surprised at the power of a regular house current? And most importantly, what did they learn in relationship to electricity?

From the day they're born, kids are taught respect for the power of electricity—to not touch downed wires, to be careful around appliances and water, and to keep children away from power outlets. And you still can't see electricity, even if you try.

God's awesome power is very similar—just as with electricity, people should fear and respect his person. From this reverential fear comes wisdom.

THE DISCUSSION, BY NUMBERS

1. Who would your kids most likely go to for advice? Take a poll of the people who they chose and why. What advice would they have for your kids that would be valuable?

2. Wisdom and respect go hand in hand. Why did your kids choose the people that they did? What makes these people trustworthy or knowledgeable? What makes your kids look up to these people?

3. How would your kids feel in this situation? In today's world many people have lost a healthy fear of God. What do most people think of God? Why might they be fearful of him? Point out that a healthy view of God includes awe and respect. God's the ultimate source for wisdom—why wouldn't they want to go to him for advice?

4. How did your kids paraphrase these verses? Ask for a few to share their verses with the group.

5. In a follow-up to question 4, how does the paraphrase of the verses apply to your kids' lives today? How would a person be affected by these verses? What tangible changes can your kids make today to model their lives after these verses?

6. Without forcing any students to share, take a general poll, to see how many of them rated themselves in the middle. Why did they rate themselves where they did? What makes them respect (or not respect) God?

THE CLOSE

God motivates your kids to serve him, but never forces them to revere him. (In the end, though, everyone will!) Loving and serving God is a choice. Point out that one mark of true godly fear is a genuine desire to be obedient to his will. God's got the best plan for each of your kids and he knows exactly what will happen every day of their lives. He may direct them in different ways and lead them down unexpected paths—but he's the ultimate authority (da man of wisdom!)

MORE

● What if your kids could ask God face to face any question they wanted to? What would they be curious about? What questions about life would they lay before him? Take some time to talk about these questions. What leaves your kids stumped about creation or life? Point out that they can ask God questions through prayer. But some answers are just too great for humans to fathom. That's probably why the answers will wait till we get to heaven!

● Some teenagers think that they can be fearless—that no one can stand in their way. You may want to talk with your group about fearlessness. What are the dangers of being fearless? What consequences occur when someone does not respect authority, nature, or others? Point out that fearlessness is naive—it is unwise and foolish because no person has the power that God has. What kids or adults do your kids know that exhibit fearless attributes? And is the degree of their fearlessness healthy or not?

CORRUPTION ABDUCTION

1. Imagine that your friends want to get you to do something. What kind of bait (food, money, stuff, people, and so on) could they use to snag you?

2. Almost everyone has heard the saying—"If all your friends jumped off a cliff, would you do it too?" What percentage of teenagers do you think probably would do what all the rest of their friends were doing?

3. Read **Proverbs 1:10-19.** How might a foolish person respond to those words? What about a wise person? Write your answers below.
   Foolish person—

   Wise person—

4. This proverb says that the people who do wrong get trapped in their own net. How can people get tangled up in traps of their own creation?

5. What do you think? Do you **A (agree)** or **D (disagree)** with each of these statements?
   ___ A person with friends who do wrong things should change friends.
   ___ A person with friends who do wrong things should try to help them do the right things.
   ___ A person with friends who do wrong things is likely to do those things too.

CORRUPTION ABDUCTION [unhealthy friendships—Proverbs 1]

THIS WEEK

Many young teens assume that they are their own person and are influenced little by their friends. Those who observe teens for any length of time have just the opposite opinion. This TalkSheet is designed to help students see that the enticement of bad friends can lead them down paths toward unhappiness and regret.

OPENER

Use your noodle! Start by putting a few dollar bills in the bait slots of several mousetraps. Then set the traps and divide your group into teams. Give each team a few uncooked spaghetti or pasta noodles. With the noodles, each team must retrieve the dollar—but without springing the traps. Use this activity as a way to introduce the first discussion question.

   Or brainstorm with your group about the different types of traps and baits—mousetraps, fishing lures, salt licks, and the like. Those in your group who hunt or fish will know a few of these. Talk about how each of them works, what kind of creature it works with, what kind of bait is used, and how likely it is that the creature will escape from the trap. How do these lures and traps compare with those (figurative) traps that people use on each other?

THE DISCUSSION, BY NUMBERS

1. Most young people know what they are likely to be tempted with. Ask them to reveal those items. Find out if your students think others are aware of their weak spots. In what different cases would your kids be tempted by different things, such as food, money, cigarettes, or drugs?

2. Allow your group to circle their best estimates, then see which students have varying opinions and the reasons for the variance. Let them defend their opinions to one another.

3. After your students have looked at these passages and commented on the possible responses, ask how many students have heard the very same responses coming from the mouths of their friends. Point out how relevant this passage of the Bible is to the present-day lives of teens.

4. Invite as many students as possible to share examples of how people they know have tangled themselves up with their own poor choices. See if your group can guess what people's mindsets might have been as they made the choices that snared them.

5. This activity will help your students to see how they can use wisdom to temper the influence of friends. Discuss the difficulties in breaking off with friends who are simply not good influences. Discuss the opportunities and dangers involved in trying to influence those friends for good.

THE CLOSE

Although many of people think people are the exception, the truth is that bad company really does corrupt good morals. We must be very careful who we choose to hang out with, because not everyone has our best interests in mind. On the other hand, God may use people to influence their friends towards good. In fact one of the greatest things a young teen can do is to draw friends toward God—but people must be strong in the faith and realize their own limitations and areas of weakness. That's the balance of giving without giving too much. Spend some time talking about this with your kids. What do they think? How strong are they when dealing with friends, peers, and family members?

MORE

● A person reaches out to others in different ways, whether as a pastor, a teacher, a singer, or a prayer-group leader. Being a witness of others for Christ is unique to each person. Challenge your kids to think of one way that they can reach out to those around them throughout the week and beyond. Dare them to go out of their comfort zones and to see what happens when God uses them in their everyday lives!

● What crowds are your kids hanging out in? Without coming off as sounding judgmental, ask your kids if they're seeking advice from wise sources. Encourage your kids to think about what they're doing and what others around them are doing. Are they fitting in or standing out? Take some time to talk about the struggles that your kids may be facing and the powerful influence of peer pressure.

CORE FOR LIVING

1. How can you tell when someone is **smart**? Pick the top five criteria from the list below and then rank those five in their order of importance for showing smarts, with 1 being the **smartest quality**.

You can tell a person is smart based on—
___ how well that person does in school.
___ how respected that person is.
___ how easily that person learns a skill.
___ how complex that person's vocabulary is.
___ how the intelligence of that person is used.
___ how many education degrees that person holds.
___ how many mistakes that person makes.
___ how many books that person has read.
___ how much money that person has made on the Internet.
___ how that person scores on an IQ test.
___ how large that person's head is.
___ how that person gets along with others.
___ how well that person does a particular job.
___ Other—

2. Have you ever really thought you were right about something, but it turned out you were wrong? Describe what happened and how you felt.

3. Read **Proverbs 3:5-6**. Write down the three most important ideas stated in the passage.

4. If you can't trust your own heart and thoughts, who or what can you trust? Check the best answer or answers.
   - ❑ Your friends
   - ❑ Internet resources
   - ❑ Your pastor
   - ❑ Media celebrities
   - ❑ Yourself
   - ❑ Your teachers
   - ❑ Your Bible
   - ❑ Your coach
   - ❑ No one
   - ❑ Your government

5. How can someone like you acknowledge God in all of your ways?

CORE FOR LIVING [trusting God—Proverbs 3]

THIS WEEK

High schoolers are in the process of making the break from home and becoming independent. Part of this process is moving away from relying on their parents' word to thinking on their own, based on other influences. More often than not, that means a group of friends, the tug of awakening senses, or the usually immature logic of their own thinking. This TalkSheet will help students to learn that God wants teens and adults alike to abandon all pretenses of wisdom and seek his ways. The reward for this sensible method is a life that remains on course.

OPENER

Create a thinking cap out of an old hat, some weird decorations, and glue. Get a hold of some fun prizes, a timer, and some trivia questions for a game of Brain Head. Have your group sit in chairs around the room, and set your timer for five minutes. When you read a question, the first person to stand may answer. If the answer is correct, this person gets to wear the thinking cap. Ask another question and if someone else answers correctly, that person gets the thinking cap. Keep this up until the timer rings, then award a prize to whoever is wearing the hat at the time. If time allows, reset the timer and start again. Use this game as an introduction to the topic of how to be a smart thinker.

THE DISCUSSION, BY NUMBERS

1. Explore what qualities define smartness to your students. List the top five they suggest. Note if there is a strong pull towards use of information or sociability—as opposed to academic achievement—as the essence of being smart (this is commonly called street smart).

2. Have several willing students share their experiences. Add an experience of your own. Point out that all people—no matter how brilliant—can be absolutely wrong at the very time people think they're right.

3. Make sure the students have identified the three ideas (trust in God with all your heart, don't rely on your own understanding, and acknowledge God in all that you do). Note that the Bible teaches that all the might of human thinking isn't to be trusted. God alone is the only one who has the wisdom to guide their lives. Ask your group what they think could result from believing it people can figure out life on their own.

4. Discuss where and how people get God's wisdom and guidance—through his Word, prayer, and the counsel of those around people (family, trusted Christian ministers, and caring friends).

5. Discuss what it means to acknowledge God in all areas of their lives. Encourage the group to come up with specific ways that they can do this. Talk about how what people say and do sends a message to others about God.

THE CLOSE

Summarize that no amount of human genius or comprehension is safe enough to use as a map for getting through this world. God's ideas, values, and directions are what it takes to walk a straight road. His words are found in the Bible and through prayer.

King Solomon was one of the wisest biblical characters. He understood that a person who is truly smart will realize that God is smarter still, and will try to discover what he has to say about the various choices facing people in life. A truly wise person will follow what God says, even if it doesn't seem to make sense at the time.

MORE

- You may want to collect videotaped interviews from people who have learned the hard way that God's way of thinking makes more sense than leaning on their own understanding. Show the interviews to your students and talk about the individual examples. What is good or bad about learning the hard way? Why does God sometimes let people mess up before they get things right? Remind them that God is all about second chances—it's never to late to get right with him and follow his wise guidance!

- How do the verses from this proverb compare to what society thinks is wise? What does the media—TV, movies, music, Internet—say about being wise and smart? What stereotypes of smart or wise people has society created? Are these fair and accurate? Take some time to talk about the media's perception of wisdom and how this affects society and your kids—and their peers.

RANDOM ACTS OF GOODNESS

1. If you knew a family was hungry and cold, when would it become your responsibility to do something about it? Check all the answers that apply.

   ❑ When they ask me to help
   ❑ When they're on my doorstep
   ❑ When they're on my street
   ❑ When they're near death
   ❑ When they're in my city
   ❑ When they're in my state
   ❑ When they're in my country
   ❑ When I know about it
   ❑ When I have lots of money

   ❑ When I become an adult
   ❑ When it's my family
   ❑ When (and only when!) it isn't their fault
   ❑ When I have everything I need for myself
   ❑ When my family members have everything they need

2. Read **Proverbs 3:27-28.** What does this verse say is the responsibility of a Christian?

3. The following is a list of things that most teenagers have the power to do. What are some practical ways that these things could be lived out?
   The power to say a kind word—
   The power to express gratitude—
   The power to listen—
   The power to help—
   The power to share—
   The power to encourage—
   The power to give—
   The power to care—

4. How can your life be different when you realize that you're accountable for what you fail to do as well as what you do?

RANDOM ACTS OF GOODNESS [good deeds—Proverbs 3]

THIS WEEK

Teenagers often are bombarded with actions or activities that are to be avoided. They are encouraged less frequently to engage in actions and activities that do good to those they have the power to help. It is these acts that spell out the reality of faith to others. This TalkSheet encourages your young people to explore options that can stretch their faith in practical ways.

OPENER

What if each of your kids could be president of the United States for one day—with the power to do all kinds of things? Have your students share what they would do if they had that kind of power at their fingertips. Some may suggest ideas that are self-serving or unrealistic—others may come up with ideas that are very positive. The point is that all of them would use the power available to them for something. Let your group know that they will be discussing how they can use the power they have right now.

THE DISCUSSION, BY NUMBERS

1. Help your young people see that the obligation to help those in need extends universally. Brainstorm ways that a young person could help someone who was hungry and cold in a faraway land. Guide them to specific ideas—such as sponsoring a child through Compassion International (www.ci.org) or World Vision (www.wvi.org), supporting church missionaries working in poor countries, and so on.

2. Discuss the answers with your group. Point out that it is the duty of every Christian to do good when the opportunity arises. But how hard or easy is it to do good? What if your friends are around or you don't have time? You may want to read the story of the Good Samaritan (Luke 10:30-36) for one example.

3. Give your students a chance to discuss and explore practical ways that they might do good with the power they have at home, at school, at work, and at church. What are some ways that they can influence people around them starting today?

4. How did your kids answer this one? What difference does it make knowing that they have responsibility? Take some time to talk through these answers with your kids.

THE CLOSE

Challenge your students to consider putting their faith into action—in small but powerful ways. They may not have people starving for food near them, but they probably know kids who are starving for acceptance and kindness. They can express thanks and gratitude to parents, teachers, and friends. And they can serve in simple ways, by washing the church van or by helping a brother or sister with stuff around the house. What practical things they can do right here, right now?

MORE

● You may want to plan a reach-out or service event with your group—maybe by cleaning a portion of the church, preparing and delivering a meal for a shut-in, or another viable project. Or look into something more long-term, like supporting a child overseas or becoming a missionary partner. For more information, check out Compassion International, World Vision, or www.YouthSpecialties.com for more links and service-related information and resources.

● Split your group up into small groups and have them check out the Bible for more verses on helping others and showing God's love. If God clearly shows that doing good is a good thing, why have people and society given do-gooders a bad rap? Why has doing good become a negative thing among some people? Point out that those who love God want to do good—out of love and gratitude to God. What attitudes are your kids mirroring to each other and to others around them?

SLACKER'S ANONYMOUS

1. How would you define **laziness**?

2. Read **Proverbs 6:6-11**. What does this passage say will happen to the lazy person?

   What example is given of the industrious person?

   What qualities does the ant display?

3. What is the right number of hours in a day for a person to be involved in the following activities? Keep in mind there are only 24 hours in a day! Write the number of hours you feel is appropriate for each activity and place a check mark by the ones you think are wasteful if done too much.

   ___ Sleeping
   ___ Being involved in sports or play
   ___ Watching television
   ___ Reading
   ___ Talking on the phone
   ___ Playing video games
   ___ Thinking
   ___ Listening to music
   ___ Hanging out with friends
   ___ Being involved in school or studies

   ___ Doing devotions
   ___ Surfing the Internet
   ___ Talking to parents
   ___ Eating
   ___ Putting on makeup
   ___ Shopping
   ___ Doing chores or going to work
   ___ Other—

4. What areas do you tend to be **lazy** in?

   What could you do to make your life more **fun** and **productive**?

SLACKER'S ANONYMOUS [laziness—Proverbs 6]

THIS WEEK

Everyone has 24 hours in a day, yet some people seem to get a whole lot done with those hours, while others barely get off the couch. One of the biblical principles to security and godliness is that of wise productivity. Young people are beginning the practices that will become habits of a lifetime. This TalkSheet is designed to help students learn to discipline and control their time so that they can not work well, but rest well, too. They can make a contribution to society and have a life that is productive by following God's principles.

OPENER

Have your students stand in the middle of the room. On a whiteboard or overhead, write the statement—I COULD GET ALL A's IN SCHOOL. Ask them to go to one end of the room if they agree with the statement, and the other end of the room if they disagree. Next, add to the statement by writing things like I COULD GET ALL A's IN SCHOOL IF I WAS GIVEN $50 FOR EACH A I BROUGHT HOME. See how many move to the agree side. Keep upping the money amount until all of the students agree with your statement, or until you are offering $100,000 for each A. Point out that if the motivation is high enough, almost everyone will work hard to get straight A's. The thing that keeps many of us from doing what we're capable of is our own laziness.

THE DISCUSSION, BY NUMBERS

1. Have your students share their definitions of laziness. Ask how they would rate themselves—are they productive or lazy?

2. Point out that an ant doesn't wait to be told what to do, but takes the initiative to accomplish what needs to be done.

3. Allow your students to explore realistic amounts of time for work, play, and rest. Point out that the time they have allowed may change as they grow older and assume more responsibilities.

4. Here is an opportunity for you to challenge your youth to break some slothful habits and to rearrange some areas of their lives. Encourage them to discuss the practical things they can think of to help with this process.

THE CLOSE

Encourage your students to be wise stewards of their time and energy. They only have one lifetime—why waste it? Point out that while television and video games may be fun, they can devour hours and even days of their lives with little practical return. Challenge them to pay their dues in hard work for anything—from playing the guitar to getting good grades—rather than thinking they will magically get the rewards for those things in the future.

MORE

● Challenge your kids to go on a multimedia fast—to give up the television, the computer, and video games for one week. Encourage those kids throughout the week via phone calls or a postcard and at your next meeting, see how many were able to achieve the goal and how they used their time. What was the hardest part about giving those things up? Ask them if their experience will make a difference in how they will approach their free time in the future. Why or why not?

● Point out to the group that there's a difference between being productive and going overboard. Today's society is stressed out! Some kids in high school are going to school, playing sports, and even working. And look at some of their parents working 50-plus hours a week! Talk with your group about the importance of relaxation and rest, along with being productive. How can your kids find productive ways to relax?

ONE IN HIM

1. What do you think causes the **most problems** in a youth group?

2. How would you rate your feelings about your youth group?

I feel very distant from this
group—it's not close at all

Our group is definitely
unified—I feel included

3. Read the following Bible verses and connect each one to the thought that represents it.

Proverbs 6:16-19   There's no place for cliques among Christians.

1 Corinthians 1:10-12   Don't grumble and find fault with each other.

James 2:1-4   We should lift up other believers by what we say.

James 4:11   God is angry with those who create problems among Christians.

James 5:9   Favoritism has no room in the Christian life.

4. How would you handle the following situations?

   • Sean doesn't like Briana. She just annoys Sean. When he can, he'll take any and
     every opportunity to make negative comments about Briana. Briana is aware
     that Sean doesn't like her, but can't figure out why.

   • The group of jocks at the church are nice guys one on one, but together their
     group is untouchable by anyone who's not part of the in-crowd. They're such a tight-
     knit group that getting to be friends with them seems impossible.

   • Sydney is a chatterbox and she'll gossip non-stop among students in the youth
     group, but she's careful to never take sides—she merely acts as the mouthpiece for
     all tidbits of gossip. A number of friendships have been damaged recently by her actions.

   • Carlos has been going to a youth group at another church down the road. He's come
     back really excited about some of the beliefs of that particular church. He knows that
     the leadership at his home church doesn't agree with these beliefs, but he thinks
     they are missing out on some important stuff. Now he's talking to other kids in the
     youth group, pointing out that their church is lame and that the other church is into
     something better.

5. How could this group become more united? What **obstacles** do you see within the
   group that keep this from happening?

ONE IN HIM [Christian unity — Proverbs 6]

THIS WEEK

Unity in the church is important. This TalkSheet focuses on problems that can lead to hard feelings and hurts within the body of Christ. It's a call for your kids to take a look at themselves—and your group—to identify behaviors that create pain for their brothers and sisters.

Be sure to keep a lid on hurtful or accusative comments or statements throughout this discussion. The purpose of this is not for your group members to bash each other—but instead to look at the unity of your group and discuss what could make it better. Don't let this turn into a gripe session.

OPENER

Try a progressive story with your group! Split your group into smaller groups (of about 6 to 10 kids each) and give each group an 8 1/2 x 11 piece of paper with one of the following headers on it (you may want to change or add some depending on your group)—

- Chase is new to town and has just started coming to your church. During one youth group meeting…
- Phong is the shy one in your youth group and hardly ever volunteers to do something, but one day…
- Adrian and Shelby, members of your youth group, are dating. They're inseparable, except when…
- Kaylee has just found out that her mom has cancer. She seems upset but…
- Zach and Gabe don't get along at all. At one youth group meeting…

Tell the first person in each group to fold the paper over so that only the first line is showing and then add the next sentence to the story. Challenge them to be creative and to think about their own group—but tell them that they can't use any names or details of people in your own group. They then fold the paper over so that only their sentence is showing and pass it on to the next person. This continues until everyone has written a sentence. At the end collect the stories and either you (or your other youth group leaders) read each story out loud to the group. Be sure to screen the stories for content that may be hurtful to a group member.

THE DISCUSSION, BY NUMBERS

1. What causes the most problems in a youth group? Take a poll of your group members to see what their responses were. What are the top three trouble spots within your group? Why? What one thing would they like to change if they could?

2. How did your kids rate themselves based on this graph? How close do they feel as a group? What has prevented them from becoming close as a group? Or what has made them become a unified group?

3. Take some time to go over each of these verses with your group. What are their responses to these verses and statements? How do these verses apply directly to your youth group?

4. Each of these situations is potentially harmful to group unity. What solutions or suggestions do your kids have? What different options does each person in these examples have? What could be done realistically to fix the relationship?

5. Discuss the ideas your kids have to create a bond of love and peace among the members of your youth group. List all the suggestions given on a whiteboard or poster board. How tangible are these solutions for your group? What can be done to get these started today?

THE CLOSE

Your students have a responsibility to keep their local church and youth group healthy, inviting, and spiritual. Point out that forgiveness, kindness, and discipline (on some occasions) are key in order to keep the group on track. If there are cliques in your group, damaged friendships, or grudges among members, those involved must be willing to forgive each other, open up to each other, and make an effort to keep the group unified. Close with a time of prayer for the unity of your group.

MORE

- Try assigning prayer partners within your group. You may want to have your kids pick names to keep things anonymous and fair. Encourage your kids to pray for and encourage each other though the next week or month. Even if they don't get along with or like their prayer partners, remind them that God wants them to pray for those people (Matthew 5:44)! You may want to debrief your group on how the prayer strengthened the group or made a difference in their relationships. And maybe continue to pick new prayer partners every month!
- You may want to plan a fun, bonding activity for your group—something that will include everyone and build their relationships. Consider a weekend camping trip or retreat. Possibly assign tasks to certain individuals, such as cooking, fire making, or clean-up. Take some time during this time for team-building activities, games, short Bible studies, and prayer.

OPEN-MINDED

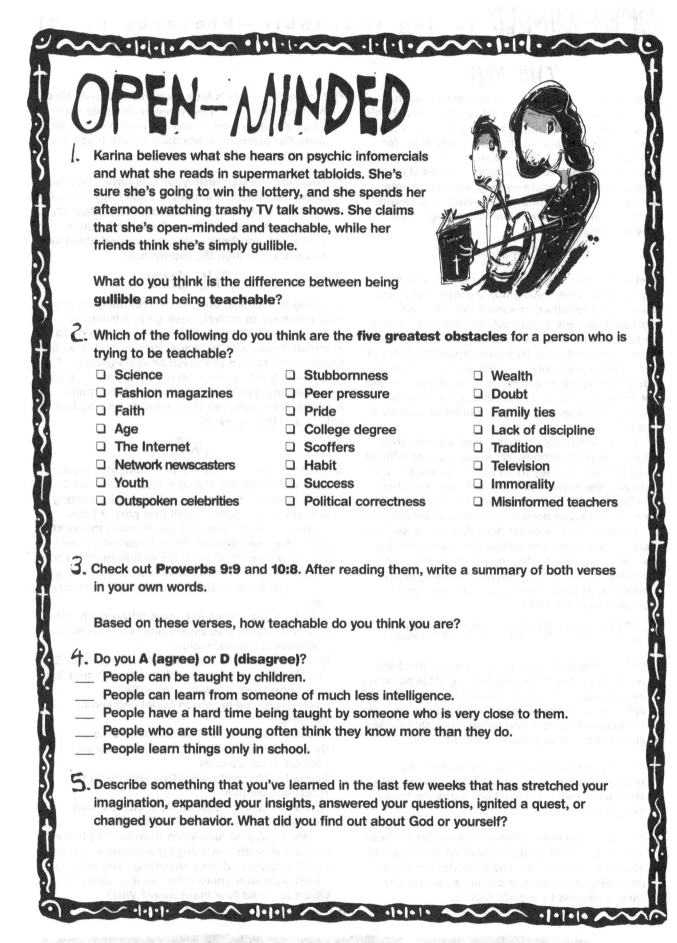

1. Karina believes what she hears on psychic infomercials and what she reads in supermarket tabloids. She's sure she's going to win the lottery, and she spends her afternoon watching trashy TV talk shows. She claims that she's open-minded and teachable, while her friends think she's simply gullible.

   What do you think is the difference between being **gullible** and being **teachable**?

2. Which of the following do you think are the **five greatest obstacles** for a person who is trying to be teachable?

   ❑ Science
   ❑ Fashion magazines
   ❑ Faith
   ❑ Age
   ❑ The Internet
   ❑ Network newscasters
   ❑ Youth
   ❑ Outspoken celebrities

   ❑ Stubbornness
   ❑ Peer pressure
   ❑ Pride
   ❑ College degree
   ❑ Scoffers
   ❑ Habit
   ❑ Success
   ❑ Political correctness

   ❑ Wealth
   ❑ Doubt
   ❑ Family ties
   ❑ Lack of discipline
   ❑ Tradition
   ❑ Television
   ❑ Immorality
   ❑ Misinformed teachers

3. Check out **Proverbs 9:9** and **10:8**. After reading them, write a summary of both verses in your own words.

   Based on these verses, how teachable do you think you are?

4. Do you **A (agree)** or **D (disagree)**?
   ___ People can be taught by children.
   ___ People can learn from someone of much less intelligence.
   ___ People have a hard time being taught by someone who is very close to them.
   ___ People who are still young often think they know more than they do.
   ___ People learn things only in school.

5. Describe something that you've learned in the last few weeks that has stretched your imagination, expanded your insights, answered your questions, ignited a quest, or changed your behavior. What did you find out about God or yourself?

OPEN-MINDED [being teachable—Proverbs 9, 10]

THIS WEEK

Some adults today think their kids aren't teachable—and that they don't want to listen. Teachable people aren't gullible people. They're people who seek out wisdom and truth in life. They think for themselves, check facts, and weigh evidence before buying an idea. Teachable individuals learn from all kinds of people—young and old, simple and intelligent. But most of all, teachable people are those willing to learn God's messages and obey his commands.

OPENER

To start this discussion, split your group up into small groups. Give each group a game to play, an object to put together, or something else that requires directions or instructions—but don't include the instructions. Need a few examples? Try a board game or a brainteaser (see www.brainteaser.com or www.brainbashers.com), or stick them in the kitchen with a few ingredients to make cookies from scratch (but no recipe). After a little while, give them the missing instructions or recipes and let them continue a few minutes.

Gather them back together and ask how they felt not having directions. What was easy or difficult about it? How did they try to figure out what to do? What was the end result? How did they feel when they finally got the instructions? What other experiences or situations have they been in when they didn't use directions, or didn't have them? Let your kids share a few stories and maybe share a story from your own experience. Then point out that the discussion topic is how to be teachable, focusing on the importance of following advice and instruction—especially from the Bible!

THE DISCUSSION, BY NUMBERS

1. What is the difference between being teachable and being a fool? Point out that a gullible person is exploitable, easily led, and has blind faith. A teachable person wants to learn but is cautious enough to check out sources and to test truth. Do your kids know friends or acquaintances like Karina?

2. Discuss the items your kids chose and why. Which ones are larger pitfalls than others? Why? Why would each of these keep someone from being teachable?

3. Your kids may have different summaries of these verses. Let a few of them share what they wrote. Then discuss what the two proverbs say about accepting commands and being eager for the wisdom shared by a godly teacher.

4. Where do your kids look for godly wisdom? Which of these items did they agree or disagree with? Why? You may want to ask for examples for each item. For example, when does a child teach a lesson to an adult?

5. What experiences have your kids have that have been "teachable" moments? What happened and what did they learn? What struck them through this experience? Let them share their experiences and ask them what they learned about God or wisdom through the experience.

THE CLOSE

Learning is a choice. Just as with learning in school, your kids have to actively seek godly wisdom in order to grow and learn. What can your kids do to stimulate learning? Challenge them to find ways of learning and to turn television or video games off. Encourage them to strike up conversations with others, including older and more mature Christians (possibly their parents!) Dare them to be question askers and truth seekers.

MORE

● Challenge your kids to do something this week to stretch their minds. Possibly find a new book to read, have lunch with an adult who's interesting to talk with, learn about a different part of town, country or world. See who can bring in the most interesting new stuff to share at the next meeting—maybe a list of fun facts or information about a topic or event. Share these with each other and encourage them to strive for new learning every day.

● Have your kids check out some different characters in the Bible who were seekers of knowledge and wisdom. For example—

⇨ Solomon—received wisdom and intuition from God
⇨ The Pharisees—tried to trick Jesus with questions they hoped he'd answer incorrectly
⇨ Paul—sacrificed his life to travel and spread the gospel
⇨ Thomas—doubted and questioned Jesus
⇨ David—sought out God for the truth and for comfort in his sorrows
⇨ Samuel—listened to what God was trying to teach and tell him
⇨ Abraham—didn't question God, but followed him fully (even with his son on an altar!)

What can your kids learn from each of these people? How did each display a different way of trying to learn and seek knowledge and wisdom? Which ones were more effective than others? Which ones did God bless more? Why?

HONESTY COUNTS!

1. Would you go to a doctor who cheated his or her way through medical school?

   Why or why not?

2. Check the following that you would consider dishonest.
   - ❑ Telling someone that your mom isn't home when she just doesn't want to come to the phone.
   - ❑ Lying about yourself on an Internet chat room.
   - ❑ Saying a friend's haircut is cool when you really think it's not.
   - ❑ Keeping the extra money that you've accidentally been given in change after making a purchase.
   - ❑ Bootlegging or copying a CD or video for your own use.
   - ❑ Passing on something that is supposed to be a secret.
   - ❑ Taking the blame for something you didn't do in order to help another person save face.
   - ❑ Taking the credit for a report you copied from another source.
   - ❑ Telling your parents you're going to the mall when you plan to meet someone there and then leave.

3. When you're dishonest, what do you worry about most?

4. Read **Proverbs 10:9**. Do you agree with the statement? Why or why not?

   Explain in your own words what you think the writer means.

5. Check out each of the Bible verses below. Then make a list of God's standards for integrity and honesty (use the back of this paper for more room).

Exodus 23:1	Psalm 37:21
Leviticus 19:11	Proverbs 14:5

HONESTY COUNTS! [integrity—Proverbs 10]

THIS WEEK

For many teens, integrity is a foreign concept with few role models. It's a lost value in their culture, where doing the right thing is dwarfed by the need to do whatever it takes to get ahead. The integrity of young teens is challenged—and compromised—daily. Will they be true to their word? Will they cheat at sports, games, or schoolwork? Will they deceive others to get out of trouble? Will they embellish events to increase their social stature? The battle to live a life of integrity never ends. Naturally, God sets high standards for integrity. But as high as they are, they are achievable and rewarding—especially when living with integrity becomes a habit.

OPENER

Play a few rounds of Balderdash! In this adapted version of the board game, Beyond Balderdash, make a list of nonsense, very obscure words—but real words nonetheless. (Just look in a dictionary, you'll find some!) A few examples from Dictionary.com (www.dictionary.com) might be—
- Coquette—a woman who flirts with a man
- Defenestration—an act of throwing someone or something out of a window
- Doppelganger—a ghostly double
- Fop—a man who is much concerned with his appearance
- Canorous—melodious or musical
- Triskaidekaphobia—fear of the number 13

You can either play as a large group or split your group up into small groups of four or five people per group. A player in each group begins by choosing a word from the categories, including words, people, objects, or any other one you want to include. All of the other players then write down a bluff, false answer to the word in the hopes of fooling each other. Shuffle the real answer in with all of the other players' phony answers and read each one aloud. A group scores points for guessing the real answer—and for also duping their peers into believing their answer is correct. Each person's task is to create a false definition for the word. Encourage your kids to try to make it sound realistic—and to be creative.

THE DISCUSSION, BY NUMBERS

1. Let your group point out the obvious—why they wouldn't trust a doctor who cheated through medical school. Throw in a few more examples, such as a president who lied to get into office, an athlete who set a world record while using illegal drugs, or a police officer who took bribes from rich crooks.

2. Allow your group to explain why some of the actions listed are dishonest or not. Be prepared to discuss what could be said that would be gentle (but still honest!) in some of these situations. Allow for some disagreement here—every situation noted doesn't necessarily have a black-and-white answer.

3. What is the downside of dishonesty? Most liars, cheaters, promise breakers, and thieves live in fear that they will be caught or discovered. Fear and guilt are not fun feelings. What do dishonest people worry about, if anything?

4. Talk about the value of a mind and heart at peace. Is there safety or security in being honest? Why or why not? What do your kids think the author means in this passage?

5. God has definite ideas and standards for integrity—but he's set a high standard because he values honesty. He does forgive human shortcomings, but he also expects that people will live lives of integrity.

THE CLOSE

Your high schoolers know that honesty really is the best policy—even when it's painful. Take some time to talk about the pros and cons of honesty—why do some people think it's easier to lie? Why is it sometimes more hurtful or harder to tell the truth? Why is dishonesty promoted in culture sometime? And why do dishonest people get away with so much? Take some time to talk about these and some other issues with your group. They may have some other moral issues and questions that they'd like to mull over with the group. Challenge them to think through their actions and words—and to see how truthful their actions are compared with their words.

MORE

- Where do your kids see dishonesty in the media? You may want to bring in a few clips of a few movies or TV shows. What do these clips deal with? What are the causes and consequences of lying? Are these examples of big lies or little ones—and is there a difference in these? Talk with your group about honesty on the Internet and in the movies. How is dishonesty glorified or promoted? How do commercials play into dishonesty? Challenge your kids to think about these questions as they watch and listen to the media through out the week.
- Ask your kids to look at some of the following verses from Proverbs on honesty—11:1, 11:3, 11:8, 12:5, 12:13, 12:19, 12:22, 14:5, 14:25, 16:13, 20:7, 20:10, 20:17, 20:21, 21:3, 21:6, 28:18, and 28:23. What do these proverbs say about the virtue of honesty? And how can your kids apply these verses in their lives today?

SINFUL NATURE

1. On a scale of 1 to 10 (**1** being **"I disagree 100%"** and **10** being **"I wholeheartedly agree"**), how would you rate each of these statements?

___ People today are less wicked than past generations.

___ People today are more wicked than past generations.

___ Only those involved in Wicca are called wicked.

___ Wicked isn't a word that's used today.

___ All people are wicked.

___ Isn't wicked the word that means awesome, like in "that's wicked!"?

___ People aren't wicked, it's just their deeds that are wicked.

___ I don't know anyone personally that I would consider wicked.

___ Wicked people are no different than anyone else.

___ Wicked people are worse than those who just sin.

2. Check out **Proverbs 10:23-25 & 27-30** and briefly jot down what will happen to the following two people.

The righteous person—

The wicked person—

3. How do you think a person becomes wicked or righteous? Pick one answer.

❑ People become righteous or wicked based on their upbringing.

❑ The choices people make determine if they will be righteous or wicked.

❑ A person is born one way or the other.

❑ God makes some people righteous and some people wicked.

❑ Wicked people are that way because they've gotten involved in the occult.

❑ People who give Christ control of their life will be made righteous.

❑ People become wicked or righteous based on who they hang out with.

❑ People can never be just wicked or just righteous—everyone is a mix of both.

4. How would you respond to the following questions—**Y (yes), N (no)** or **U (undecided)**?

___ Is it right for Christians to judge actions or people as wicked?

___ Is it right for Christians to attempt to stop some kinds of wickedness?

___ Is it right to use force to stop some forms of evil?

___ Should Christians try to convince the wicked that they really are wicked?

5. What do you think is the difference between **wickedness** and **sinning**? Is one worse than the other?

SINFUL NATURE [human wickedness—Proverbs 10]

THIS WEEK

Wickedness is hard to define in today's society. What is the difference between wickedness and sin? Some define wicked people as those involved in Satan worship, those who commit vicious crimes, or those who deliberately turn against God. Wilson's Old Testament Word Studies says, "Wicked men are those who pursue that which is vain and false with lawless desire, casting off the fear of God, and so come at length to trouble and sorrow" (Hendricksons, 1993).

The human condition is sinful—it lies deep in the heart of people, including your kids. And the Bible clearly states that a person in rebellion from God is wicked. How do your kids perceive wickedness in the world today? Do they equate wickedness with sin? Could they identify wicked behaviors in their own lives? Use this discussion to talk about the different ideas or understandings about wickedness and its influence on those who are Christians.

OPENER

Start off by asking your group to nominate people for the dark honor of being the most wicked human being to walk the face of the earth. You might get a wide array of choices, including biblical characters, figures in history, or current individuals. What makes each of these people wicked? What qualifies them to be one of the most wicked? What have they done that makes them so awful? Select the top five candidates with your group and take a vote for the person they think is the most wicked human ever to walk the earth. What caused the wickedness in this person?

THE DISCUSSION, BY NUMBERS

1. How did your kids rate each of these statements? Take a poll of their ratings and discuss with your students the various ideas floating around about wickedness. Note that people often reserve the word *wicked* for the very worst of humans. In fact many of them can't even think of a person they know personally who they would call wicked.

2. What do these verses say about a wicked person? Ask for your kids to share what they jotted down. What do these verses say about the eternal results of righteousness and of wickedness?

3. How do people become wicked or righteous? What truths or errors do your kids see in some of these statements?

4. How should Christians respond to wickedness? Ask your group to share their answers and discuss the pros and cons of each question. You may want to let your group members debate any disagreements with each other.

5. What can your kids do to personally solve the problem of human wickedness? What do they think the difference is between sin and wickedness? Point out that all people are sinful—it's part of being human. Wickedness may mean something else to your kids. Talk about how your kids understand wickedness versus sin.

THE CLOSE

Wickedness is a reality—our culture is permeated by it, TV shows glorify it, and music lyrics exalt it. It can be simple rebellion against God—not just horrible deeds committed by the worst of humans. But how can your kids battle wickedness in their own lives? If your kids don't already have Christ in their lives, invite them to make him the Lord and Master of their lives. Point out that being a Christian doesn't shield them from sin. Living for God requires perseverance and strength. God is the one that can give them unconditional love and forgiveness when sin and wickedness get in the way.

MORE

● The media flood teenagers with messages of wickedness. They don't have to look far to see it in the world around them. Point out that people are like sponges—their minds soak up what they see and hear (you can illustrate this with a sponge and colored water). Visual images and lyrics stick in their minds. Some people are so saturated by evil that nothing else can get in—they're defiant of Christianity and consumed with the sin in their lives. Whether they know it, your kids are being pressured and influenced by the sin around them. Have they noticed this in their own lives? Do they listen to what they hear on the radio? Are they actively discerning what they see on TV or on the Internet?

● The Bible is filled with examples of wickedness—and God's response to and punishment of it. You may want to split your kids into groups and give each group a passage below to read and discuss. Ask them to identify the evil behaviors and the consequences of the wickedness. Afterwards talk about each passage with the group to summarize what God thinks of wicked behavior.

⇨ Genesis 4:3-16
⇨ Genesis 9:1-29
⇨ Numbers 15:40-41; Numbers 16:1-50
⇨ Joshua 7:14-26
⇨ 2 Samuel 11:1-27; 2 Samuel 12:13-19
⇨ 1 Kings 16:30-33; 1 Kings 19:1-2; 1 Kings 21:25-26; 1 Kings 22:35-38; 2 Kings 9:32-37
⇨ Hosea 5:4; Hosea 9:9; Hosea 9:15; Hosea 12:14

WINDOW TO THE SOUL

1. Which of the following items deal with the **outside of a person (O)** and which deal with the **inside (I)**? Do any deal **with both (B)**?

___ Strength   ___ Patience   ___ Agility
___ Courage   ___ Self-control   ___ Imagination
___ Faith   ___ Muscles   ___ Humor
___ Beauty   ___ Generosity   ___ Intelligence
___ Creativity   ___ Godliness   ___ Honesty
___ Kindness   ___ Attractiveness   ___ Friendliness
___ Style   ___ Ugliness

2. What do you think the average person is most concerned about—the **outside** appearance or the **inner** self?

3. Read **Proverbs 11:22.** Check which of the following you think best describes the symbolism used in the passage.
   ❏ Pretty women make better wives than pigs.
   ❏ A person who is beautiful on the outside but impure and foolish on the inside is a sad waste.
   ❏ Don't waste gold on a dirty pig when you can use it as a wedding ring.
   ❏ A woman with no discretion will hang around with pigs.
   ❏ Pigs and people with no sound judgment are the same.
   ❏ Beautiful people should have wise judgment and pigs shouldn't wear jewelry.

4. Read these statements and decide if they're **T (true)** or **F (false)**.
   ___ A majority of people put more work into how they look than who they are.
   ___ A beautiful person can also be ugly.
   ___ A person who is good looking will get further in life than someone who isn't.
   ___ A person who is attractive on the outside will probably be attractive on the inside as well.

5. Check out the following passages. Then in your own words, write down the important qualities for true beauty described in these verses.
   Matthew 5:8   Ephesians 4:22-24   Galatians 5:22-23

From *High School TalkSheets Psalms and Proverbs—Updated!* by Rick Bundschuh and Tom Finley. Permission to reproduce this page granted only for use in the buyer's own youth group. www.YouthSpecialties.com

79

WINDOW TO THE SOUL [inner beauty—Proverbs 11]

THIS WEEK

Teenagers are bombarded by a world of attractive and desirable images. Many fail to recognize the need to put at least an equal amount of time and effort into developing their inner character. The writer of Proverbs equates a jewelry-wearing pig (an animal unclean to the Jews) with a person who is attractive on the outside but ugly on the inside. This TalkSheet offers an opportunity to talk with your students about working on their characters, their spiritual lives, and their personalities with the same fervor that they work on their outside appearance.

OPENER

Ask your kids to describe what makes a person beautiful (or handsome, or "hot," or whatever), according to what society thinks today. Write down their suggestions on a white board or poster board. Who formed or created these ideas of beauty? How much are people judged by these standards? Are your kids judged by these standards? Do they judge others by these standards? Why or why not? Are these ideas and standards healthy to live by? Why or why not? Which ones are okay to use as standards? What would God think of these standards?

THE DISCUSSION, BY NUMBERS

1. Ask your students to explore which of the attributes are external or internal in nature. Allow for debate and disagreement. Which can be both (such as strength, attractiveness, beauty, and ugliness)? Which ones are more emphasized than others?

2. Have a few willing students share their answers. If the group is honest, most will admit that average people worry more about their outside package. Talk about what creates that focus—the images that are held up to people through the media and the fragility of their own self-images.

3. Ask for a few students to share their answers. Make sure they've identified the correct answers (the second and the fifth). Point out that a pig was considered an unclean animal to the Hebrew writers who compiled these proverbs.

4. Use this quiz to stimulate discussion about people who look attractive—but whose thinking is mixed up. Encourage the group to look past the surface—there are those who may not match society's standard of beauty on the outside but have inner qualities and gifts that can take them a long way in life.

5. Help your group to describe these biblical qualities for inner beauty in their own words. You may want to ask how these qualities can be seen in people today and invite them to affirm such qualities that they see in one another. Point out how these can get better with age—unlike physical beauty!

THE CLOSE

People, and society, are consumed with outward beauty. Some people find this sickening. And although you won't dissuade your kids from spending time in front of the mirror, you can remind them that it is entirely possible to be drop-dead gorgeous, but have an utterly unattractive character. Give them the straightforward fact that God looks only at the heart and—because the body is a shell—who people are will last forever. That's why God wants people to invest in their inner qualities. Brainstorm some ways that your kids can work on their character—or at least how they can balance it out with the time they spend on their appearances. Challenge them to think about making a commitment to spend more time with God during the week, to improve a friendship or family relationship, to volunteer their extra time, or something else.

MORE

● Using the discussion from question 1, you may want to make a two-column list of the characteristics of external beauty and inner beauty. Then compare these two lists and decide with your group how concerned people their age are about the characteristics in each column. Why are people so focused on their outside selves but not worried about the violence, vulgarity, and anger in the world today? Why do they think so many girls their age have become victims of eating disorders and depression? Give your kids time to think about these and other questions that they might have.

● You may want to spend some more time talking about God's views of beauty—and explore some other verses on the topic—1 Samuel 16:12; 1 Samuel 16:18, Psalm 27:4, Proverbs 31:30, Ezekiel 28:17, 1 Peter 3:3-5a, 2 Timothy 3:1-5. What do these verses say about beauty? What does God say or value about beauty in these verses? How would he want these verses reflected in the lives of your kids—girls and guys—today? What do they think God thinks of beauty? In which context—internal, exterior, or both?

GIVE OR TAKE

1. Circle the last person you bought a gift for with your own money.

Mom	Friend	Uncle
Dad	Girlfriend or boyfriend	Grandma
Brother	Teacher	Grandpa
Sister	Pastor	Self
Neighbor	Aunt	No one

2. What is **one gift** that you would like to give if you could afford it. Who would you give it to and why?

3. Check out **Proverbs 11:24**. What doesn't appear to make sense in this verse?

What could the answer be?

4. Match these passages with what they have to say about being a giver.

Proverbs 22:9	People should give with a cheerful attitude.
Matthew 6:1-4	The person who is generous will be blessed by God.
Acts 20:35	People should give quietly and secretly.
2 Corinthians 9:7	Giving really is better than receiving.

GIVE OR TAKE [generosity — Proverbs 11]

THIS WEEK

High schoolers sometimes struggle between being takers and being mature, generous givers. Some are making money and paying for their own cars and clothes. Others are still relying heavily on their parents for financial support. During this time, they'll develop an attitude toward giving that will affect them the rest of their lives. Giving doesn't mean money alone—it includes actions and time! This TalkSheet will discuss generosity and what it means to give even when they are flat broke.

OPENER

What would your group members do in these situations? Challenge them to think honestly and realistically about their responses.

- You're always sharing your stuff with your sister, who is three years younger than you. Because you have a job and make money, you buy more clothes, CDs, and stuff. You were trying to be generous, but now you think your sister is taking advantage of you.
- You leave the theater with some friends and pass a beggar on the street. He asks you for extra change, but all you have is a $10 bill.
- Your pastor says that you should tithe 10 percent of what you make. But you're only making minimum wage at a burger joint and need the money!
- Your grandpa likes to hand over extra money to you—after all, you're his favorite grandkid (or so you think!) Sometimes he gives you $50.
- Your school is hosting a food and clothing drive for a nearby mission organization. They ask if you'll volunteer an hour or two to help out.

What does each of these situations say about generosity? How would your group members respond to each of these? Point out that some are healthy examples of generosity and some aren't. Take a few minutes to talk about their responses.

THE DISCUSSION, BY NUMBERS

1. Ask for some willing students to share their answers. When do they buy gifts for others and why? When was the last time they went out of their way to buy someone something? How often do they buy themselves stuff compared to buying others stuff?

2. Invite your students to discuss who they would give the gift of their dreams to and why. How would it make them feel to be able to give such a gift? Why?

3. Discuss God's strange (but functional!) economy— To give is to gain, to die is to live, to be last is to be first. Ask your students to brainstorm how

these principles might apply in modern, real-life situations.

4. Ask the group to sum up what it means to live a life of godly generosity. How do these attributes apply to their own lives? Encourage them to give specific examples or share stories from their experiences.

THE CLOSE

Wrap up by asking about the benefits of being a giver. How are others affected by our generosity? How does giving change the person who gives? What happens when giving people give too much? Or when the takers take too much? Talk about balancing giving with taking. Then challenge your group to follow up on the ideas they brainstormed in question 6. Finally, is there something that you as a group can do together to show your generosity?

MORE

- You may want to—if your kids are interested—pick names anonymously for secret supporters. Then for a week, two weeks, a month, or more, these people can secretly support and encourage each other by giving small gifts, a letter, or even just prayer. Maybe do it this for a special event or holiday. Either way, follow up with your group and ask them how it felt to give and to receive. What was easier or harder? And how did they feel when they gave and didn't receive (or vice versa?). Why is it hard to give unconditionally?

- You may want to talk about the paradox of giving in a society like America. With all the advertisements, shopping malls, and Internet shopping, it's no wonder that kids are saturated with the "take all-have all" mentality. How can your kids survive in this culture and maintain or develop a giving nature? What can they do to keep themselves and others from getting caught up in wanting it all? How much do they get from their parents? And are they giving anything back?

DID YOU HEAR?

1. If you something private that you wanted to tell to one person, who would you tell?
   - ❑ Best friend
   - ❑ Parent
   - ❑ Youth pastor
   - ❑ Boyfriend or girlfriend
   - ❑ Teacher
   - ❑ Brother or sister
   - ❑ Grandparent
   - ❑ Stranger in an on-line chat room
   - ❑ Coach
   - ❑ School counselor
   - ❑ The class gossip
   - ❑ Other—

2. Have you ever had someone tell others something you had said in confidence?

   If yes, how did it make you feel?

   How did it change your relationship with the person you told the secret to?

3. For which secrets below would you break the confidence of a friend and tell someone else? Why?
   - ❑ Your friend tells you about a secret crush.
   - ❑ Your friend says she is pregnant and is considering abortion.
   - ❑ Your friend confesses to cheating on the English final.
   - ❑ Your friend tells you something he's ashamed of doing.
   - ❑ Your friend tells you that a family member is sexually abusing her.
   - ❑ Your friend confesses to experimenting with drugs.
   - ❑ Your friend admits to considering running away from home.
   - ❑ Your friend confides in you about being HIV positive.
   - ❑ Your friend tells you he's thinking about suicide.

4. Check out these verses and paraphrase each one in your own words.
   Proverbs 11:13

   Proverbs 17:9

   Proverbs 20:19

   Ephesians 4:29

From *High School TalkSheets Psalms and Proverbs—Updated!* by Rick Bundschuh and Tom Finley. Permission to reproduce this page granted only for use in the buyer's own youth group. www.YouthSpecialties.com

83

DID YOU HEAR? [gossip—Proverbs 17]

THIS WEEK

Some young people have a lot of secrets. And for some, nothing is as fun as leaking a juicy tidbit from someone else's life. Gossip is a national pastime in our culture. Adults, young people, and the media seem to revel in gossip. Although gossip is sometimes interesting, it can destroy reputations and tear apart friendships. This TalkSheet will help your group discover that only some things need to be shared with others and that keeping a confidence will strengthen friendships and build trust between people.

OPENER

There's no better example of gossip than the media tabloid. You may want to purchase a couple of these at any supermarket and select two or three articles to read to your group. Ask your students to vote on which stories they think are true and which they think are false. What makes a story believable? Why or why not? And why do people buy into these stories and false lies about others? Discuss what sells those tabloids. You may want to rewrite one of the stories using the names of some of the young people in your group, then talk about what it feels like to have these kind of stories written about oneself.

For Internet tabloid sites (so you don't have to be seen buying one!), check out Tabloids.com (http://4tabloids.4anything.com), the National Enquirer (www.nationalenquirer.com), or Star Magazine (www.starmagazine.com).

THE DISCUSSION, BY NUMBERS

1. Who would your kids be most likely to trust with a secret? Why they would trust the person? What makes this person trustworthy?

2. Discuss the feelings that come when a confidence has been violated. Have a few willing students share what happened to them, and what the betrayal by their friends did to their relationship (no specific names!) Point out that gossip and betrayal destroys and damages relationships, including relationships with friends, within marriages, and even with God.

3. Which secrets would a real friend absolutely not keep (suicide threats or sexual abuse, for example)? Why or why not? What other secrets are okay to reveal? Be prepared for a lot of disagreement on some of these issues. Point out the potential harm that comes from not telling someone else if a friend is keeping a harmful secret.

4. Have a few willing students share their phrases (being trustworthy, betraying a confidence, promoting love, and so on). Talk to your students about the impact that breaking a confidence has on friendships, trust, and their integrity as Christians.

THE CLOSE

Human beings are funny creatures—people love the tidbits of scandal and the lure of knowing something that others would rather keep private. But this causes people to be focused on anything but the essentials of being honest, truthful, and real with others—and with God. Encourage your kids to keep a careful ear open for what they hear and to become discerning listeners as well. They can choose what to believe and what not to believe. And they carry the responsibility of what to remember and pass on to others. How would they want others to handle their deepest secrets?

MORE

- You may have some kids in your group who are holding some secrets that are eating them inside—possibly an abusive parent, failing grades, the lure of drugs or sex, or more. These are real issues that need real attention. Pay close attention to your kids during this discussion and let the group know how crucial it is to talk with a trusted adult. For more information check out www.YouthSpecialties.com for more links to sites on issues in teens' lives including rape, abuse, pregnancy, suicide and more. Or see Soul Pollution (47) or The Perfect Parent (27) for more links and discussion items.

- God isn't a fool. He knows what is going on in the lives of your kids and their friends. You may want to check out these other passages with your group—Psalm 44:21, Jeremiah 20:12, 1 Chronicles 28:9, Jeremiah 17:10, Proverbs 21:2, Psalm 27:14, Psalm 112:8, or 1 Thessalonians 3:13. These verses clearly show that God knows your kids' hearts and is working in their hearts. How do your kids feel knowing that God knows their secrets—before they even tell him? How do they feel knowing that God examines their heart every day? Challenge them to get real with God and bring their fears and concerns to him. He's their greatest, most trusted friend—whether they know it or not.

LIVID OR LET GO

1. **Who was the last person you lost your temper with?**
   - ❑ A brother or sister
   - ❑ A teacher
   - ❑ A parent
   - ❑ A friend
   - ❑ A kid my age
   - ❑ An animal
   - ❑ A member of the opposite sex
   - ❑ A stranger
   - ❑ Other—

   What happened?

2. **What's the difference between being angry and losing your temper?**

3. **Rate the ways people react when they lose their temper, from the worst (1) to the not so bad (10).**
   - ___ Slam doors or throw things
   - ___ Scream and yell
   - ___ Get mad at people who have nothing to do with the situation
   - ___ Clench fists, grind teeth, bulge eyes, and breathe hard
   - ___ Say hurtful words
   - ___ Cry
   - ___ Hit, slap, scratch, or push somebody
   - ___ Destroy property, commit crimes
   - ___ Use foul language and curses
   - ___ Do nothing and keep it inside

4. **Do you think a temper is controllable? Why or why not?**

5. **Check out the verses below and number them from 1-7 (with 1 being most important) in order of their importance for Christians.**
   - ___ Proverbs 12:16
   - ___ Proverbs 15:1
   - ___ Proverbs 15:18
   - ___ Proverbs 16:32
   - ___ Proverbs 19:19
   - ___ Ephesians 4:26
   - ___ James 1:19

LIVID OR LET GO [controlling your temper—Proverbs 12, 15, 16, 19]

THIS WEEK

Some people's tempers are worse than others'. Some people handle their anger in different ways. Teenagers often see—and experience—tempers in adults, who should have brought them under control long ago. This TalkSheet will give your students an opportunity to examine how they react to disturbing situations and to discuss what kind of behavior and self-control they should strive for.

OPENER

Start off by asking your group to rate how they would react to each of these situations. Ask them to rate each on a scale of 1 and 10 (1 being "It wouldn't upset me at all" and 10 being "I'd be so mad, I'd be dangerous"). Situations you could list include someone insulting you; someone insulting your mother; someone beating up your friend; someone beating up your five-year-old brother; someone breaking something and then blaming you; someone cussing you out; someone cutting in on you on the freeway; or someone dumping you. Ask them to list other situations and how they would rate them. Feel free to add to the list and to make the situations as serious as you'd like. Keep a poll of their ratings on a white board or poster board. What is the most common rating of responses? Why do some react differently than others? Are the girls more upset at some situations—or are the guys?

Or ask your group to bring in examples of songs that express anger or rebellion. Play the song or read the lyrics and talk about what the anger is and how the person could deal with it. What does the song say about anger? What is the singer angry about? How is the anger handled, well or badly? You can also look for lyrics on the Internet at www.mp3.com.

THE DISCUSSION, BY NUMBERS

1. Continue the dialogue you've started by discussing the last time your students lost their tempers and why. Discuss over what and why they lost their cool. You may want to share a situation where you lost your temper and why—and how you felt afterwards.

2. What's the difference between being angry and losing your temper? Point out that even Jesus was angry at times! Help your students to distinguish the difference.

3. Point out how much damage can be done when people blow up in anger. Ask your students to share how they react when other people lose control of their temper. What reactions are worse than others? Why or why not?

4. Ask for some of them to share their answers. Can people control their tempers or not? Is there a point where everyone loses their ability to control themselves?

5. What do these verses say about anger? How did your kids rate these verses in order of importance? Which verse is the most important for Christians? Why? Which verse applies most directly to the lives of your kids today?

THE CLOSE

Anger is a human emotion—it's okay to feel irritated and angry from time to time. But controlling anger means having self-control. Some people lack the self-control to stop themselves before they blow it and hurt someone. Point out that self-control is a fruit of the spirit. Help for dealing with anger isn't too far away. God gives peace and he gives self-control. Challenge your kids to try the 10-second anger test. If they feel irritated, silently stop and count to 10—slowly. Then think about how they're reacting. Are they willing to let God give them self-control—or will they go ahead and blow their top?

MORE

● Some of your kids may experience anger-spouting situations firsthand. You may have kids in your group who have been hurt, yelled at, or hit by their friends, siblings or parents—or have seen a sibling or parent become victims of anger and violence. If you sense situations of physical abuse among your group members, take note of it, and encourage your kids to talk with an adult. Communicate that under no circumstances is it okay for a parent to beat a child or another family member. For more information on domestic violence and abuse, check out Child Help USA (www.childhelpusa.org) or the American Humane Association (www.americanhumane.org), The Family Violence Prevention Fund (www.fvpf.org), or Christians In Recovery (www.christians-in-recovery.com).

● What other characters in the Bible dealt with anger? You may want to break your group up into smaller groups and let them find examples of anger in the Bible. A few of these include Job (who didn't get angry with God), Jesus (who got angry in the Temple), Judas Iscariot (who got so angry at himself that he killed himself), and even God himself (who got angry and destroyed Sodom and Gomorrah). Talk about these and more examples with your group and how this relates to their lives today. What lessons on temper can be learned from these characters?

ONE TRUE THING

1. Do you **agree** with this statement? Why or why not?
   It doesn't matter what you believe as long as you're sincere.

2. List something that you once believed was true, but now you don't believe is true.

3. How many of your friends would agree
   with the following statements—
   M (most), S (some), or **N (none)?**
   ___ If it's in the newspaper or on TV, it
       must be true.
   ___ If it makes sense, it must be true.
   ___ If your teacher says it, it must be true.
   ___ If everyone else believes it, it must
       be true.
   ___ If it's in the Bible, it must be true.
   ___ If it's on the Internet, it must be true.
   ___ If your parents believe it, it must be true.

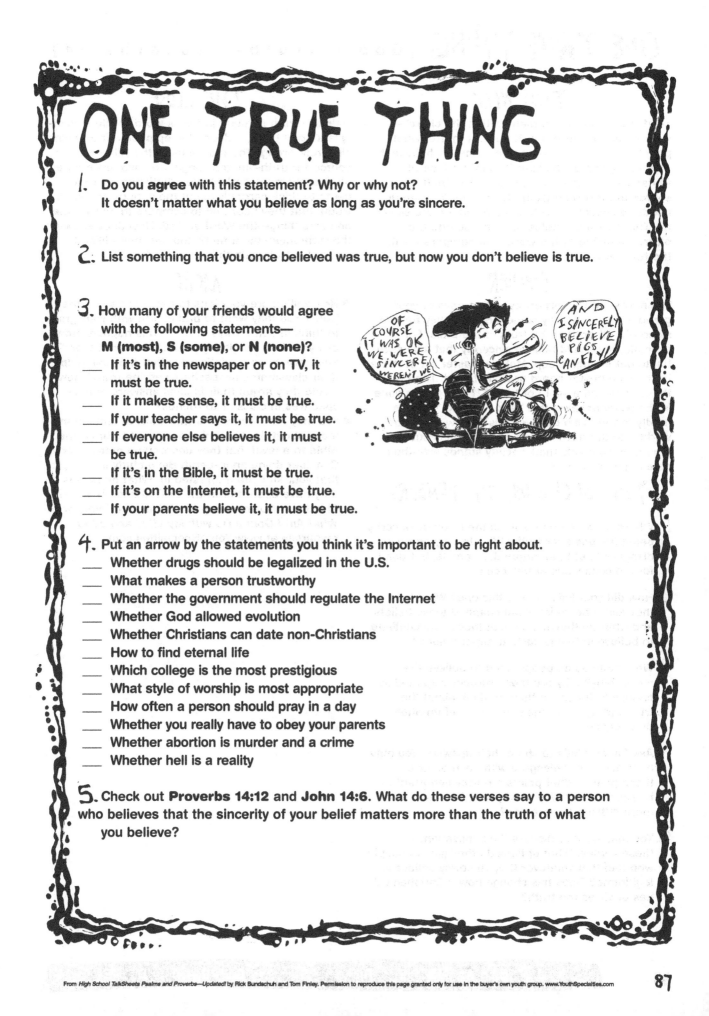

4. Put an arrow by the statements you think it's important to be right about.
   ___ Whether drugs should be legalized in the U.S.
   ___ What makes a person trustworthy
   ___ Whether the government should regulate the Internet
   ___ Whether God allowed evolution
   ___ Whether Christians can date non-Christians
   ___ How to find eternal life
   ___ Which college is the most prestigious
   ___ What style of worship is most appropriate
   ___ How often a person should pray in a day
   ___ Whether you really have to obey your parents
   ___ Whether abortion is murder and a crime
   ___ Whether hell is a reality

5. Check out **Proverbs 14:12** and **John 14:6**. What do these verses say to a person
   who believes that the sincerity of your belief matters more than the truth of what
   you believe?

ONE TRUE THING [God's truth—Proverbs 14]

THIS WEEK

Most teens—including many within the church—would quickly affirm that it doesn't matter what people believe as long as they sincerely believe it. This faulty line of thinking flies in the face of Christ's words proclaiming himself to be the only source of life-giving truth (John 14:6). Your group needs to know that truth is more than mere sincerity. This TalkSheet helps them probe into the blurred thinking of the world and compare it with the teaching of the Bible.

OPENER

You may want to start off by asking each of your group members to say something that they believe sincerely, other than the truth of the Bible. For example, one could believe sincerely that it's essential to get enough sleep. Make a master list of these truths on a poster board or white board. Then rate these truths on a scale of 1 to 10 (1 being "Everyone in the world believes this" and 10 being "There's hardly anyone who believes this"). How would the world rate the truth of God and his son Jesus? Where do your kids think society stands with the sincere belief in Christ?

THE DISCUSSION, BY NUMBERS

1. Where do your kids stand on the issue of sincerity being the basis for truth? Why do they agree or disagree? Let them argue their points, but don't form a consensus at this point.

2. How did your kids answer this one? What have they lost a belief in? What changed those beliefs and what do they think about those who continue to believe in things such as superstitions?

3. What sources do people tend to believe the most? Why? Why are these sources regarded as credible? Challenge them to think about the trustworthiness of the sources of information they rely on.

4. Ask for your kids to share their answers. You may have some that disagree with each other on these points. What points are truly important to be right about? Why or why not? Why are some more difficult to agree on?

5. You may want to discuss the implications of these verses. What options do they give to people who feel that whatever they sincerely believe is legitimate? Does this change how a Christian values or views the truth?

THE CLOSE

Ultimate truth is found in God's Word. While sincerity is a good thing, it doesn't keep people from being sincerely wrong. The teachings of the Bible are our source for truth—its teachings are solid, even if people find them uncomfortable. Challenge your students to think carefully about the various so-called truths that they hear and to compare them with the one true thing—the Word of God. How does knowing the truth make them feel? And are they willing to share this truth with those around them?

MORE

● How willing are your kids to help others see the truth? You may want to brainstorm with your group to think of some ways to make this happen. How can your kids tangibly get God's word out there? What are some realistic ways that they can help their classmates or teachers see the truth? How would they argue their biblical answers or perspectives in class or to friends?

● You may have some kids who want to understand more about the truth. You may want to bring the Bible to a level that they understand more clearly. Consider doing an in-depth Bible study on a topic that your kids are interested in. What questions do they have about the truths of God and his word? Check out *Downloading the Bible, Good Sex, or So What Am I Gonna Do with My Life?* and other resources at www.YouthSpecialties.com.

TRUTH OR CONSEQUENCES

1. What percentage of truth would you give of each of these items—**all, none, or 1/2?**

    ___ Money makes everything in life easier.

    ___ There's no right or wrong to controversial issues.

    ___ Angels are real in the lives of humans.

    ___ Earthquakes and wars prove that God is coming back soon.

    ___ Truth is what you perceive it to be.

    ___ Friends are the biggest influence in the lives of teens.

    ___ Study time determines the grades you get.

    ___ Choices you make today will affect your future.

    ___ People are better Christians today than they were in the past.

    ___ Satan really isn't that powerful.

    ___ Some sins don't have direct consequences.

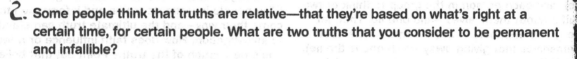

2. Some people think that truths are relative—that they're based on what's right at a certain time, for certain people. What are two truths that you consider to be permanent and infallible?

3. If you didn't believe in God, what would you put your faith in?

4. **Check out Proverbs 14:15.** What is the definition of a simple person and a prudent person?

5. Kayla has been struggling with the beliefs of Christianity. She has some serious questions about the truth of it. She's brought up some of these doubts to a few of her friends, who've told her to quit questioning and just have faith. Now she's feeling lost.

    Is it okay for Kayla to be questioning her beliefs? Why or why not?

    How would you respond to her doubts if you were her friend?

    Does doubting your faith make you less of a Christians? Why or why not?

TRUTH OR CONSEQUENCES [intelligent Christianity—Proverbs 14]

THIS WEEK

In an era of relativism, teenagers struggle to find truth in their lives. Some of your kids may be dealing with some serious doubts and questioning their lives and beliefs. And they're flooded with different answers from different sources. How can they know and find the truth? This TalkSheet will encourage kids to become thinkers, to check facts, and to seek truth.

OPENER

You may want to start off this discussion by—

- Asking your kids to bring in a piece of information that they found on the TV, Internet, or in a magazine or newspaper. Challenge them to bring in a fact or two that no one else in the group would know. It can either be a true or false piece of information. Let the group share their bits of info and let the rest of the group vote and debate to decide which one is true or false. Was it easy to tell which ones were true or false? Why or why not? Which pieces of information surprised your kids?

- Playing a version of the previous game, but with information from your kids' own lives or experiences. For this game (known as Two Truths and a Lie), ask each person in the group to think of two truths about themselves—and one lie. Then let the group members share the three facts about themselves (not giving away which one is the lie). See if the rest of the group can discuss which one is the false one. How hard was it to figure out the lies? Why or why not? Did they make their assumptions based on the person—or what they knew about the person?

- Or if you don't have time to play either of these, bring in some information yourself. You can easily find information anywhere on the Internet. Check out some of the news Web pages, such as USA Today (www.usatoday.com), Newsweek (www.newsweek.com), People (www.people.com)—or some tabloids (for the false facts?) the National Enquirer (www.nationalenquirer.com), or Star Magazine (www.starmagazine.com).

THE DISCUSSION, BY NUMBERS

1. What percentage of truth did your kids give each of these statements? Take a poll of your group to get their responses. Which students doubt most of the statements? Which believe most?

2. What truths do your kids consider to be permanent and infallible? Ask them for examples of why they gave these choices. How can they decide which truths are relative and which aren't? How does being a Christian influence the truth in a person's life?

3. Where would your kids turn if they didn't know God? What about their friends or family members who don't know God? Talk about these with your kids and ask them why people look to some of these sources for the truth. What makes them dependable or trustworthy?

4. How did your kids interpret these verses? Discuss what it means to be simple and what it means to be prudent in God's economy. How do simple people—and prudent people—determine the truth? Which do your kids perceive themselves to be—simple or prudent?

5. It's not uncommon to struggle with one's beliefs—and question Christianity. How would your students respond to Kayla? Is it okay to question or doubt God or their faith? Why or why not? How does questioning or doubting weaken or strengthen one's faith? Take some time to answer questions that your kids may have about their faith or any doubts that they're dealing with.

THE CLOSE

Remind your kids that their minds are gifts from God. Wise people investigate truths and information that come their way—and the ultimate truth can stand up to investigation. How does faith influence or affect one's perception of the truth? Point out that believing in God and loving him means trusting him alone. Finally, let your students know that being prudent (rather than simple) involves mental and spiritual effort. How easy or difficult is it for your kids to be prudent? What challenges them in this area? You may want to spend some time talking through some doubts or issues that your kids may have.

MORE

- Many biblical characters questioned the truth about God. You may want to have your kids check out the following verses (or look for more) and discuss them with the group—Genesis 3:1-6; Genesis 17:15-22; Genesis 18:10-15; Judges 6:14-23; Luke 1:5-20; John 18:33-39; and John 20:24-29. What was the character doubting or questioning? Did this relate to their faith in God and how? What were the consequences (either good or bad) of their doubting? What does this say to your kids about doubts and God's will?

- You may want to talk more about how to address the situation in item 5. How would your kids explain the truths of the Bible? Which truths are hard to explain or prove? What aspects of Christianity do your kids struggle with? You may want to have a Q&A session to discuss these with your group—and encourage them to find Bible verses to back up their answers or ideas.

HOW GREAT I AM

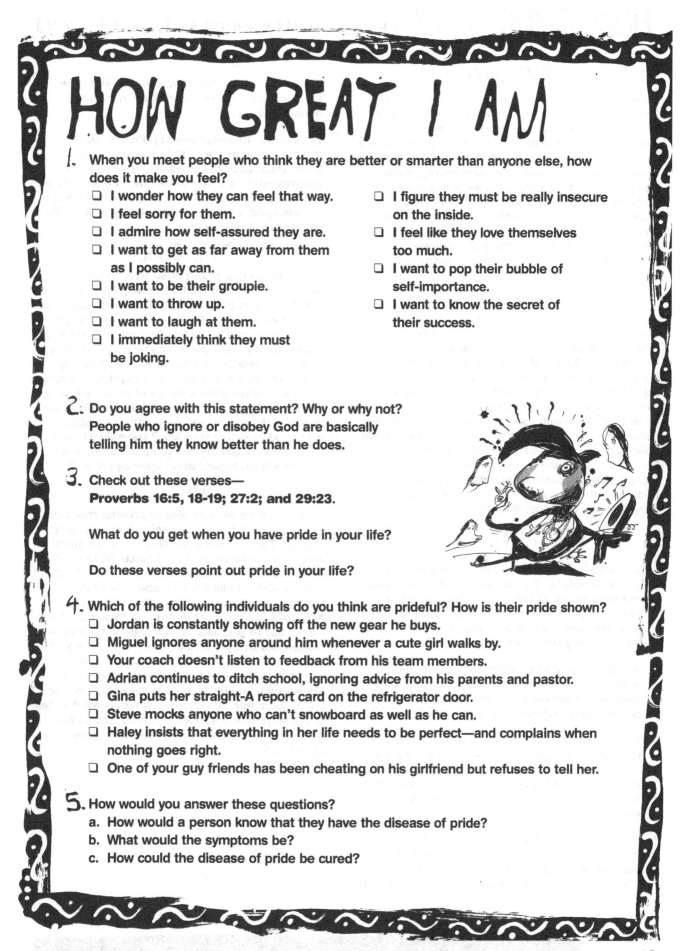

1. When you meet people who think they are better or smarter than anyone else, how does it make you feel?
   - ❑ I wonder how they can feel that way.
   - ❑ I feel sorry for them.
   - ❑ I admire how self-assured they are.
   - ❑ I want to get as far away from them as I possibly can.
   - ❑ I want to be their groupie.
   - ❑ I want to throw up.
   - ❑ I want to laugh at them.
   - ❑ I immediately think they must be joking.
   - ❑ I figure they must be really insecure on the inside.
   - ❑ I feel like they love themselves too much.
   - ❑ I want to pop their bubble of self-importance.
   - ❑ I want to know the secret of their success.

2. Do you agree with this statement? Why or why not?
   People who ignore or disobey God are basically telling him they know better than he does.

3. Check out these verses—
   Proverbs 16:5, 18-19; 27:2; and 29:23.

   What do you get when you have pride in your life?

   Do these verses point out pride in your life?

4. Which of the following individuals do you think are prideful? How is their pride shown?
   - ❑ Jordan is constantly showing off the new gear he buys.
   - ❑ Miguel ignores anyone around him whenever a cute girl walks by.
   - ❑ Your coach doesn't listen to feedback from his team members.
   - ❑ Adrian continues to ditch school, ignoring advice from his parents and pastor.
   - ❑ Gina puts her straight-A report card on the refrigerator door.
   - ❑ Steve mocks anyone who can't snowboard as well as he can.
   - ❑ Haley insists that everything in her life needs to be perfect—and complains when nothing goes right.
   - ❑ One of your guy friends has been cheating on his girlfriend but refuses to tell her.

5. How would you answer these questions?
   a. How would a person know that they have the disease of pride?
   b. What would the symptoms be?
   c. How could the disease of pride be cured?

HOW GREAT I AM [pride—Proverbs 16, 27, 29]

THIS WEEK

Every person is tainted by pride to some degree. Some think pride means bragging or self-glorification—but it's also found hidden in attitudes, like wanting to make fun of others or feeling that nobody can tell one what to do. Pride is most destructive when it challenges God, and many young people do—passively. They simply ignore him, even while professing to believe. The cure to pride is humility—the realization that one isn't any more special than anyone else and that people are all equal before God. This TalkSheet will help your students to define pride, to understand its destructive power in their lives, and to explore its cure.

OPENER

Start out by asking your kids to share an example of pride—to list all the words or phrases they think describe or reflect pride. What characteristics of pride have they observed in their friends or in people at school? Write these examples and phrases on a whiteboard or poster board for the group to see. Then go through them with your group and rate them on a scale of 1 to 10 (1 being very prideful and 10 being not prideful at all). Then ask your group when pride becomes a bad thing. Where is the line between feeling good about yourself and being too proud? Why is pride harmful to relationships and friendships? Then jump into the TalkSheet discussion.

THE DISCUSSION, BY NUMBERS

1. Talk about how it feels to encounter people who are very prideful. Do your kids think these people are even aware of their pride? Why or why not? What's the difference between people who boast because they are insecure and people who boast because they think they are superior?

2. Ask for a few willing students to share their answers. How do they think God feels about these situations? Point out some subtle forms of pride such as resistance, stubbornness, and quiet rebellion.

3. What do these verses say about pride? Discuss the results of sinful pride—both temporary and eternal. How does God view pride? And how does pride affect Christians and how they reflect God to others? What pride do your kids see in their own lives?

4. Explore which actions your students think are prideful and which aren't. Are some of these people more prideful than others? Why or why not? You may get some disagreement—ask students to

defend their answers or arguments. Based on these examples, what could be a working definition of pride?

5. What would the symptoms of pride be? What were their opinions or answers to these questions? Refer them back to the biblical examples—a haughty spirit, a boastful tongue, and an attitude of disdain. Point them also to the cure for pride—a lowly spirit, an attitude of humility, and a willingness to do without.

THE CLOSE

Point out to the group that pride puts distance between a person and God. Prideful people set themselves up as their own supreme authority—they become their own god. On the other hand, people who have the humility to obey God are blessed and rewarded by him. And those who have the humility to see others as worthy and valuable end up having more friends than those who are too prideful. Explain how Christ dissolved the barriers of pride by eating with social outcasts, hanging out with so-called sinners, and picking common people for his disciples. How is pride affecting your kids? Have they hurt a friend, parent or God by being too prideful? How does it feel to be looked down upon by others?

MORE

● There are several examples of prideful charaters throughout the Bible. Take some time to check each of these verses out with your group members—Deuteronomy 8:11-14; 2 Kings 20:12-18; 2 Chronicles 26:16-21; Esther 3:1-6; Daniel 5:18-21; John 11:45-53; Luke 18:11-14; and Acts 12:21-23. How did the character show his or her pride? What was the result of their pride? What do these verses say to your kids about pride in their lives?

● Sometimes being proud comes from the lack of accountability to others. Some parents don't notice the pride in their kids—others ignore it. Challenge your kids to hold themselves and others accountable about pride. You may want to talk about ways that your kids can hold themselves, their friends, parents, and others accountable against pride.

THERE FOR YOU

1. Read the questions and decide what do you think.
   Is it **easy** or **hard** to make friends?
   Is it **easy** or **hard** to keep friends for a long time?
   Is it **easy** or **hard** to break apart a friendship?

2. If you were able to download the perfect friend by selecting qualities on a Web site that are important to a friendship, which **five** of the following would you pick? Circle them.

Similar interests	Popular	Wealthy	Kind
Loyal	Truthful	Outgoing	Generous
Funny	Spiritual	Christian	Clean
Smart	Trustworthy	Creative	Cheerful
Athletic	Honest	Humble	Courageous
Able to keep	Good-looking	Easygoing	Responsible
secrets	Same age	Witty	Industrious
Musical	Same race	Patient	

3. Check out the following Bible passages. What does each passage say about friendship?
   Proverbs 17:17
   Proverbs 18:24
   Proverbs 27:6
   Proverbs 27:9-10

4. Read the statements and then whether they're **T (true)** or **F (false)**.
   ___ A friend will never tell you what you don't want to hear.
   ___ A friend will stick with you no matter what.
   ___ A friend can be closer to you than a relative.
   ___ A friend will try to prevent another friend from making a bad choice.
   ___ Two friends will like the very same things.
   ___ A friendship can be worn out by too much togetherness.
   ___ A Christian would be sure to tell his or her friends about Christ.
   ___ A Christian should only have Christian friends.

5. If you were to write a short sentence in an article about your best friend, what would you say? What would you want said about you by your best friends?

THERE FOR YOU [friendship—Proverbs 17, 18, 27]

THIS WEEK

Friendships are the heart and soul of the teenager years. As friendships become more and more important, your high schoolers are learning what creates and sustains valuable and lasting friendships. They'll learn what kind of friendships to cultivate as well as what kind of friendships and friends to avoid—and what kind of friend they need to become. This TalkSheet will help the students to discover that friends can be one of the greatest gifts that God gives them.

OPENER

Your kids have most likely learned about friendship through television shows and movies. You may want to start off by showing a few clips of TV shows or movies that portrays friendship. Chose a variety of examples, including same-sex friendships, group friendships, and mixed-gender friendships. Ask your kids to observe the friendship shown. In the opinion of your kids, how healthy are the friendships portrayed? Why or why not? Was there a disagreement or conflict—and if so, was it valid? How did the two (or more) people relate to each other? How did same-sex friendships differ from girl-guy friendships? Talk about the perception of friendship from these examples and how realistically your kids think these situations were handled.

THE DISCUSSION, BY NUMBERS

1. Talk about the process of making and keeping friends. Discuss what might cause friendships to dissolve and what can make friendships last a long time. Why do people shift and change friendships? Is this a good thing or a bad thing? When do friendships change the most in a person's life? Why?

2. Discuss the qualities of a real friend. Which qualities are the most desirable to have and why? What makes a friend a true friend? Do any of your kids have friends that have these qualities?

3. Have a few willing students share their answers (a friend loves at all times, loyalty is important, you can trust a real friend, you don't run out on your friends, and so on). Talk about the ideas the Bible contributes to the area of friendship. Discuss why a friend telling you bad news is better than flattery from an enemy, and why friends are important to have for advice and help.

4. Discuss myths and fallacies about friendship. Some of your kids may have both Christian and non-Christian friends. Talk about the pros and cons of having friends like them. How does this affect them at school or at church? You may want to talk about their opportunity and responsibility to share Christ with their unsaved friends.

5. Ask your group to share what they would say about a friend as a tribute in an article. What would they say and why? How does this compare with what they'd want said about them? What's hard about doing this activity? Why? How often do your kids let their friends know that they value and appreciate them?

THE CLOSE

Friendships take work, patience, and wisdom in order to last. Point out to your kids that everyone is different. Some people are better at making friends than others and some people will have more friends than others. Some people are happy with a few close friends while others like to have lots of friends.

You may want to talk about some of the famous friendships in the Bible like David and Jonathan, Jesus and his disciples, and Paul and Timothy. How are these examples of godly friendships? What characteristics of friendships were shown? How did these friends help each other and support each other?

MORE

● You may want to talk more about friendship in the media—on TV, in movies, song lyrics, magazines, and so on. How do these portray friendship as opposed to what this proverb talks about? You may want to bring in (or have your kids bring in) articles, song lyrics, or clips of a TV show or movie. Talk about society's views of friendship versus God's views of friendship. How do these compare? What is the value of friendship, based on these sources?

● Challenge each of your kids to encourage a friendship or two this week—to send a friend an e-mail or note, hang out with them, or something else. Maybe brainstorm some ways that your kids can work on their friendships. Then have them pay attention to how the friendship changed or grew from these efforts. Was it easy to work on the friendship? Why or why not? How did the friend react?

TO TALK OR NOT TO TALK

1. Imagine that you've just inherited a slew of money. You want to invest it so that when you're older, you'll have enough for a college education, a new car, or a house. Who would you go to for advice on what to do with your money? Why would you go to this person?

2. Have you ever heard a person speak as if he or she were an expert on a subject, when in reality the person knew little about it?

   What were your thoughts about the person and what he or she was saying?

3. Check out **Proverbs 18:2**. What do you think the proverb is talking about?

4. What five **subjects** or **areas** are you knowledgeable in?

5. Everyone seems to have an opinion on one subject or another—look at the talk shows on TV! What's the danger or harm of speaking out about a topic or issue that you know little about?

   Does this damage a person's reputation? How so?

   How about the reputation of a Christian? Why or why not?

TO TALK OR NOT TO TALK [speaking wisely— Proverbs 18]

THIS WEEK

Everyone has an opinion. Some people—teenagers included—state their ideas on all kinds of things that they know nothing about. Godly wisdom, however, teaches people to seek understanding, insight, and knowledge. It teaches people to listen more than they talk. Just because people have the ability to express their opinions doesn't mean they always need to. This TalkSheet session will help your students see that while everyone has opinions, not everyone is entitled to make it public.

OPENER

On a whiteboard or poster board, make a list of topics or issues. Include a variety of items such as effective studying techniques, communicating with the opposite sex, decision-making skills, budgeting and money management, raising a child, choosing a career, driving a car, dating and marriage, or maintaining a healthy diet. There are all issues that your kids will most likely have to deal with sooner or later. On a scale of 1 to 10 (1 being "I know everything there is to know about this, so don't question me" and 10 being "I don't know squat, so don't ask me"), how do your students rate their knowledge level for each item listed? How would they rate the knowledge level of their parents? How does a person learn about these things? Are some people more knowledgeable than others?

THE DISCUSSION, BY NUMBERS

1. Who would your kids go to about a money question? Why did they choose this person? What makes this person knowledgeable? Why did some of your kids choose different sources for advice?

2. Ask for a few willing students to share their examples. What are these people doing to their reputations by talking about things they don't know about? How do they look to others? How does it make them—and those around them—feel?

3. How did your group members interpret this verse? Discuss what makes the person a fool—the lack of motivation to truly understand a situation and an urgency to give one's own opinion about that situation.

4. Ask your students to share areas in which they have some degree of authority and knowledge. Compare their strong and weak areas. Did any of them list Bible knowledge as a strong area? Why or why not? Why do some people have different strong areas than others?

5. What would your kids say to someone who talks but doesn't really know anything? Discuss ways to respond when they're asked an opinion about something that they know little or nothing about. Why do some people act like they know a lot when they really don't? Why do people today think they have a right to give an opinion on something they don't know much about?

THE CLOSE

Point out that your group members will often hear others giving an opinion on things they know little or nothing about. This is particularly true when it comes to the Bible. They'll hear ideas and opinions about the Bible, Christ, God, heaven, hell, or salvation or from people who've never read the Bible. God wants people to speak wisely, to seek understanding and information rather than reacting blindly—he wants people to know what others are talking about. Challenge your kids to think about what they know before giving an opinion—and to challenge themselves to learn more about what they don't know.

MORE

- You may want to split your group into small groups and have them pick a passage from the Bible that they're not familiar with—maybe from a book in the Old Testament. Ask them to read the verses as a group and brainstorm what it means for Christians today. You may want to offer them suggestions of passages or stories. Then regroup and have the groups share what they read and learned. Point out that the best way to get closer with God—and to understand him better—is to spend time reading what he wrote to his people!

- What sources of advice do your kids see in society and the media today? Where do most people go for helpful, constructive advice? An Internet chat room? A psychic hotline? Talk about foolish ways to seek advice in society. How useful as educational tools are the TV or the Internet? What are the dangers or risks of misusing them? See how your kids interpret the info they get from the media and how this affects their wisdom.

YOUR REPUTATION AND YOU

1. What **three words** would you pick to describe your reputation?

2. Do you agree or disagree with this statement? A solid reputation takes time to build, but can be destroyed in an instant.

   Why or why not?

3. Check out **Proverbs 22:1**. How does this passage apply directly to you?

4. Put an X by **five** of the items below and briefly describe how each item could either strengthen or damage a person's reputation.

   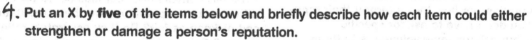

Being a liar	Being forgiving	Being boastful
Being opinionated	Being aggressive	Being peaceful
Being prejudiced	Being self-centered	Being hardworking
Being kind	Being cautious	Being loyal
Being carefree	Being humble	Being honest
Being creative or imaginative	Being proud	Being self-controlled
Being a gossip	Being moral	Being immoral

5. What do you think? Pick two of the questions below to answer in your own words.

   In what ways can a person **benefit** from having a good reputation?

   In what ways can a person **suffer** when she has a bad reputation?

   In what ways can a person **suffer** when he has a good reputation?

   In what ways can a person **benefit** when she has a bad reputation?

YOUR REPUTATION AND YOU [reputation—Proverbs 22]

THIS WEEK

Teenagers want to be liked, admired, and accepted. Most of them base their worth on their reputation—they dress for the approval of their peers, act out roles for the applause of their peers, and hurt when they're rejected. A solid reputation is important and valued by teenagers. This TalkSheet discusses developing a positive reputation and the takes effort and struggles involved.

OPENER

Start by bringing in some newspapers or magazines. Toss them on the floor and pass out a few pairs of scissors. Then ask your group to find and cut (or rip) out advertisements that tie in a certain product with a person's reputation. What does the advertisement say about a person's reputation, appearance, or acceptance by others? Let your kids share their examples with each other and talk about why a reputation would be important to consumers. Why do people buy into advertisements that promise to fix a person or improve a reputation? What other examples do your kids have? How affected do they think they are by the media and its advertisements?

THE DISCUSSION, BY NUMBERS

1. What three words did your kids pick to describe their reputation—or how they interpret their reputation? You don't have to ask for specific answers, but ask for some volunteers to throw out words that some may have picked—based on cliques at school or a particular social status. Make a list of these words on a whiteboard or poster board. Are these words positive or negative? Are they based on society and what others think—or what God thinks?

2. Did your kids agree with this statement? Why or why not? Talk about the process of building or damaging a reputation. You may want to share a time when someone's reputation was hurt (maybe you, a friend, or someone in the media). What caused the problem and what did it take to repair the reputation?

3. The Bible gives high value to a good name or reputation. How high would the price tag be if a person had to purchase a good reputation? Ask for a few volunteers to share how they interpreted the verse.

4. Some of these characteristics or habits could enhance or destroy a reputation. Some could do either. Go over each one to see what your kids think. Could a characteristic be positive or negative in different circumstances or with certain people?

5. Ask for some volunteers to share their ideas. You may want to make a list of their responses on a whiteboard or poster board. Point out the benefits of a good reputation—being trusted, being someone others come to for help and advice, gaining the respect of peers, and so on. What are the benefits of having a bad reputation, if any? Why do some kids with bad reputations become more popular than others?

THE CLOSE

It's important for your kids to put effort into living lives that will give them a good reputation—but they have to be honest with themselves, too. Words and actions go hand-in-hand with one's character. Do the reputations of your kids reflect their characters? What kind of reputation are your kids after? Will this reputation hurt them in the end or not? Would they like to change their current reputation? You may want to discuss ways to repair a reputation and how to start over, including being willing to forgive others. Encourage them to start over with God and ask him for the strength to live for him.

MORE

- Those with certain reputations have nicknames. What nicknames have your kids heard for those with a certain reputation? Are these reputations and nicknames fair? Do they accurately reflect the person? Point out that nicknames are sometimes cruel ways of labeling people. Encourage your kids to look at others beyond the nicknames—and to reconsider the nicknames that they give to others.

- What are some characteristics of a godly reputation? You may want to go through the Bible with your kids, or split them up into small groups, to look for examples and words that describe a Christ-like reputation and character. Point out that Jesus didn't have a good reputation with some people because he helped those in need, hung out with sinners, and healed the weak. Sometimes it's not easy to have a godly reputation—God doesn't promise that it'll be easy. What characteristics do your kids need or want to work on? And are they willing to stand up to those who mock or challenge their beliefs?

GIMME, GIMME

1. If you had a wish that would come true, would you wish for lots of money? Why or why not?

2. What's the largest amount of money (your own money!) you've ever spent at one time? What did you spend it on?

3. What do you think is the biggest **danger** in wanting lots of money? Rank the following from the **greatest danger (1)** to the **least (10).**

___ Cheating or stealing to get money
___ Ignoring other priorities to make money
___ Becoming consumed by greed
___ Spending too much of it once you have it
___ Not investing your earnings wisely
___ Becoming addicted to gambling
___ Worshiping money more than God
___ Thinking you don't need to depend on God any more
___ Getting lots of money but no happiness
___ Using friends or family members to get money

4. Read **Proverbs 23:4-5** and **Luke 12:15-21**. What do these two passages say about the desire to get rich?

5. If there was a master list of important things in your life, where would the desire for money fit in?

Lowest Priority   **Highest Priority**

GIMME, GIMME [greed—Proverbs 23]

THIS WEEK

By now, your high schoolers have discovered the power of money! They're working for it and spending it. Many have bought into the idea that happiness and money are directly related. But the Bible is clear on the topic of striving for wealth. It warns kids and adults alike that the minute they fix their gaze on the dollar, it sprouts wings and flies away. This TalkSheet session is designed to help your students to see that material gain is the wrong place to put their focus, and that real eternal treasure is made up of things that don't disappear.

OPENER

Start by presenting the following scenarios (or more you've thought up) to you group—
• It's time to find a summer job. For one job you'll work 30-plus hours a week and make over $10 an hour, but the work is boring and you know the time will drag. The other job is really fun, but you'll be working 50-plus hours and making barely enough to get by. Which job would you choose?
• It's time to accept an offer to a college or university. One is very prestigiousand offers a very large scholarship—but it doesn't have the program that you want to study. The other prestigious school, has the program you're interested in, but will require you to take out thousands of dollars in student loans. Which one would you choose?
• You're finally ready to buy a car! You're debating whether to pay more for a brand new car that looks great, but will cost a bundle in insurance—or a car a few years older, that's less stylish but affordable.

Which options did your kids choose and why? You may want to list of their reasonings and priorities for choosing what they did. Have their parents had to deal with these situations? What do they think most people in the world do in this situation? Use this discussion as an opportunity to introduce today's topic.

THE DISCUSSION, BY NUMBERS

1. Would your kids wish for money? Why or why not? What would they wish for instead?

2. Ask for a few willing students to share their answers. Do any of them have regrets about money they've spent in the past? What did they buy? Was it worth it or not?

3. How did your kids rank these items? Which ones did they rate the most dangerous and why? How would their relationship with God be affected?

4. What do these verses say about wealth? How do these verses apply to your kids' lives? You may want to have them rewrite these verses in their own words and to insert their own examples. Then have a few of them share what they wrote.

5. Allow your students to determine where the desire to get money sits on their priority list. Where on the graph should a warning flag go? What can your kids do to keep a godly perspective on money?

THE CLOSE

Society is consumed with material things and living the good life. It's important for teenagers to keep their guard up so they don't get sucked into the gimme mentality. Point out that this is hard, especially in a country so focused on advertisements, shopping malls, and more. Encourage your students to make it a priority to invest in things that can't be taken away—their faith in God, their relationships with others, and who they are as a person. Challenge them to bring their needs and desires to God and to trust him with their wants.

MORE

● How do advertisements affect materialism and consumerism? Ask your kids to make a list of everywhere they see advertisements—on clothing, on buses, on the Internet, and even on cereal boxes. Where do they see advertising? How does advertising influence people to buy things they don't need? How can your kids keep advertisements from getting to them? You may want to show a few videotaped commercials and talk about the messages that are given.

● How do your kids spend their money? Challenge them to keep track of everything that they spend money on in a given week and write it down. Then talk with them about what they bought and whether or not the items were things they needed or wanted. They'll be surprised to see how they've spent their money!

BE A LIFESAVER

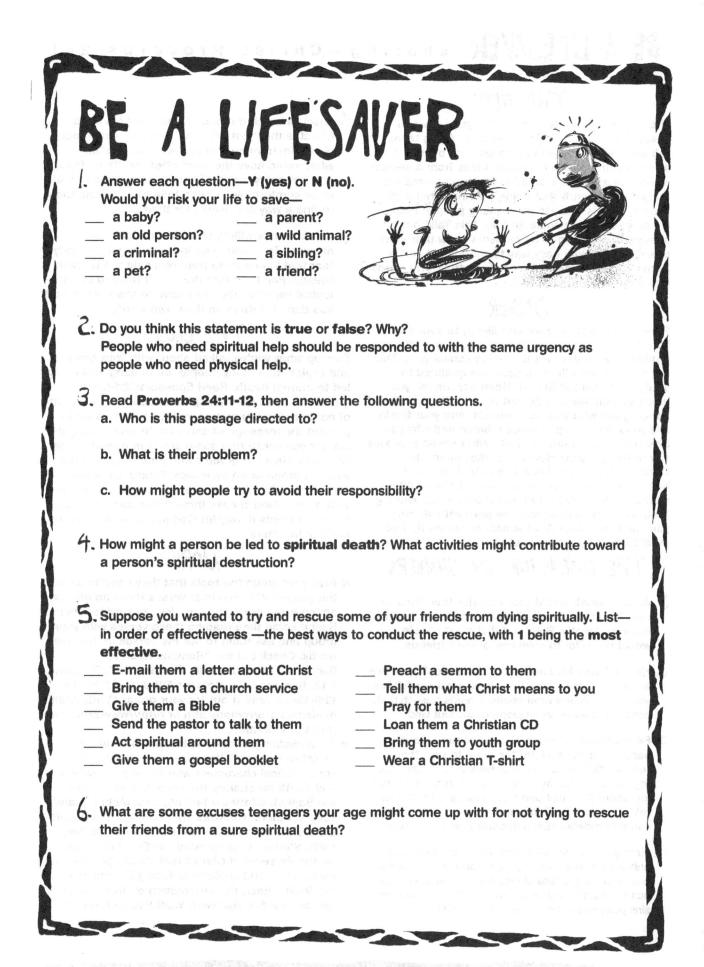

1. Answer each question—**Y (yes)** or **N (no)**.
   Would you risk your life to save—
   ___ a baby?   ___ a parent?
   ___ an old person?   ___ a wild animal?
   ___ a criminal?   ___ a sibling?
   ___ a pet?   ___ a friend?

2. Do you think this statement is **true** or **false**? Why?
   People who need spiritual help should be responded to with the same urgency as people who need physical help.

3. Read **Proverbs 24:11-12**, then answer the following questions.
   a. Who is this passage directed to?

   b. What is their problem?

   c. How might people try to avoid their responsibility?

4. How might a person be led to **spiritual death**? What activities might contribute toward a person's spiritual destruction?

5. Suppose you wanted to try and rescue some of your friends from dying spiritually. List— in order of effectiveness —the best ways to conduct the rescue, with **1** being the **most effective.**
   ___ E-mail them a letter about Christ   ___ Preach a sermon to them
   ___ Bring them to a church service   ___ Tell them what Christ means to you
   ___ Give them a Bible   ___ Pray for them
   ___ Send the pastor to talk to them   ___ Loan them a Christian CD
   ___ Act spiritual around them   ___ Bring them to youth group
   ___ Give them a gospel booklet   ___ Wear a Christian T-shirt

6. What are some excuses teenagers your age might come up with for not trying to rescue their friends from a sure spiritual death?

BE A LIFESAVER [sharing—Christ Proverbs 24]

THIS WEEK

The commission to tell others the good news of Jesus Christ has no age boundaries. Young teens rub shoulders daily with those who are being led away to spiritual death by false ideas from a secular world. Christians are called to the rescue—but the obligation to gently (but boldly!) share Christ with their friends is scary to most young people. Heck, it's scary to most people, period. This TalkSheet session is designed to let students know that there is an effective and easy way to share what Jesus Christ means to them personally, in their own words and their own ways.

OPENER

Present this scenario (or one like it) to your kids. Your family has decided to host a foreign exchange student from India for the coming school year. This person is an excellent student and qualified to study in the United States. Upon her arrival, you discover that she is a devout Hindu. After months of hanging out with you, your friends, and your family, she asks you to explain your religion and why you love this God person so much. What would your kids say to this person? How would they share their Christian faith with this person who has never heard one word about Jesus Christ before? What would be the hardest or easiest part about sharing their faith? How does this compare with sharing your faith with friends at school or others that you meet? Which situation would be easier? Why?

THE DISCUSSION, BY NUMBERS

1. Who, or what, would your kids risk their lives to save? Take a poll to tally the answer they marked most frequently. Point out that most people would risk a lot to save one of their friends.

2. How did your kids answer this question? How are spiritual needs as important as physical needs? Help your group define what spiritual needs are—that students' very souls are in jeopardy without God.

3. Be prepared for some strong reactions to this passage. It will be hard for some to face their responsibilities. Some may have a hard time facing up to the reality of hell. Spend some time talking about this. But don't use hell as a threat—a relationship with God is more than that, it's a personal friendship with someone who loves them.

4. Help your group understand how the everyday, unhealthy activities that people can fall into—obsession with money, sexual temptation, and so on—can actually lead to a slow spiritual death. How do these sins pull people further away from God?

5. Discuss which method of telling others about Christ is the most effective. Let your young people brainstorm on this and ask your students what would have the most effect on them. Point out that everyone is different—some people feel more comfortable sharing than others. Help them to find a way that works for them.

6. Ask for a few willing students to share their answers. Help young people see that it's usually fear that keeps them from reaching out to their friends. Point out that they don't have to be theological experts—they just have to share what God has done for them, in their own words.

THE CLOSE

Sum up what you've talked about with your group and explain that many people are in danger of being led to eternal death. Read Ephesians 2:1-5 with your group and point out that spiritual death is the result of not knowing Christ personally. You may want to present the message of salvation to your kids, especially if you sense that some aren't in a relationship with God. Give the group some time to pray either with the group or on their own. Finally, challenge them to ask God for the strength and words to share with others. God speaks through his spirit! He'll give them the words if they let God use them for sharing his love to others.

MORE

● Give your group the tools that they need to share the gospel—the essential verses they can use as ammo when presenting the love of God to others. Spend some time reading these verses with your group and ask them to put the verses in their own words. Check out the "Romans Road to Salvation"—Romans 3:10, Romans 3:23, Romans 5:12, Romans 6:23, Romans 5:8-9, and Romans 10:9-13—or print it out for your group at http://hmi-ministries.org/romans.htm or http://www.pfbaptist-press.org/29.htm.

● What challenges stand in the way of sharing Christ with others? You may want to talk about some biblical characters who faced persecution and death for sharing the gospel, such as John the Baptist, (Matthew 14:1-12), Paul (Acts 14), and several others (Hebrews 11). Point out that people around the world today are persecuted for their faith. *Student Underground: An Event Curriculum on the Persecuted Church* realistically portrays the persecution and challenges facing Christians in the Middle East. For information on this curriculum or to order, visit www.YouthSpecialties.com.

EVEN MY ENEMY?

1. Who would you consider to be your **worst enemy**, if you have one?

2. Check the top **three ways** that you think people deal with their enemies.

- ❏ Put them down whenever possible.
- ❏ Help them out if they are in need.
- ❏ Physically hurt them.
- ❏ Think about ways to hurt them.
- ❏ Cuss the person out.
- ❏ Talk to them on the phone.
- ❏ Try to get them into trouble.
- ❏ Threaten their friends.
- ❏ Sabotage their locker.

- ❏ Send them anonymous, harsh e-mails.
- ❏ Pull a gun on them.
- ❏ Spread rumors about them.
- ❏ Dislike their friends and family, too.
- ❏ Look for ways to bless them.
- ❏ Talk to them kindly.
- ❏ Ignore them.
- ❏ Pray for them.
- ❏ Hope they die a slow and painful death.

3. Check out **Proverbs 25:21-22; Matthew 5:43-48;** and **Romans 12:14.** What specific instructions do these passages give about how people should treat their enemies?

4. What would your enemy do or say if you treated him or her as Christ commanded?

5. If treating their enemies the way Jesus commanded is the goal for Christians, how successful are you in reaching that goal? Mark your position on the line below.

Failing miserably   **Always like Jesus**

EVEN MY ENEMY? [loving your enemies—Proverbs 25]

THIS WEEK

Through movies, TV shows, and violence in society, teenagers have learned to deal with enemies in a manner far different than that required by Jesus. Most students will struggle with the plan God lays out for dealing with enemies—they can't imagine how it would help them. This TalkSheet session provides a great opportunity to challenge students to see if they really trust God enough to follow his commands, even when they seem bizarre.

OPENER

What is the most common way that enemies relate to each other? How does the media glorify enemies—and how to deal with them? You may want to ask your kids to list examples of how people in society deal with their enemies (from the least to most extreme), from enemies of state (world leaders versus world leaders or country versus country) down to personal enemies (friends, relatives, and so on). What is the general message that society gives to those who hate an enemy? If you feel it's appropriate, you may want to share a few different examples of how someone dealt with an enemy. Possibly show a movie or TV show clip or read an article from a magazine or from the Internet. Ask for your kids' reactions to these situations. Were they surprised or shocked? Why or why not? What are the consequences of the actions taken against the enemy? How will these affect others?

THE DISCUSSION, BY NUMBERS

1. What makes a person an enemy? Ask for a show of hands to see how many of your group members have people in their lives who they would consider to be real enemies?

2. Talk about the way people treat those who they think of as enemies. You may want to ask which of the ways seem crazy and why. How does society in general treat enemies?

3. How would your students describe the treatment the Bible says people must give to their enemies? Discuss how this contrasts with the way people usually treat those they dislike.

4. Have a few willing students share their answers. Some might say that any enemy would think they were weird or strange. Then ask them this—how would you react if your enemy treated you as Christ commanded?

5. Why is loving our enemies a hard order for most people? Where are your students in their ability to practice what the Bible teaches on this subject?

THE CLOSE

Explain to your group that it's difficult—but not impossible—to care for those who hate us. Let them know that this process is done one step at a time, starting with something simple such as refusing to say bad things about the person. Once they've succeeded at little things, they can go on to other gestures of peacemaking. Encourage them to ask God for help in dealing with their enemies and to ask him for the strength to love the enemy back. Challenge them to pray for one enemy during the week and to see what happens—does the relationship improve? Why or why not? What is God teaching them about love, patience, and perseverance?

MORE

● Ask your students to rewrite Matthew 5:43-48 by substituting for the word *enemy* the name of a person who they would consider their enemy for the word enemy. What does this verse say to them? Is this verse an encouragement to them or not? How do these verses relate with being a Christian?

● How did some biblical characters handle their enemies? You may want to take a look at some of these stories and examples. Check out the relationship between Jesus and Satan (Matthew 4:1-10), Jacob and Esau (Genesis 27:41), Esther and Haman (Esther 7), David and Goliath (1 Samuel 17:1-54), or Joseph and his brothers (Genesis 37). How did God work in these relationships and what happened? Note how God used the bad for the good—just as he can with enemies today.

COMING CLEAN

1. Do you think it's easy to cover up something wrong that you've done? Why?

2. What are the **top five reasons** people cover up the things they do wrong?
   - ❑ They're afraid that others will think they are weird.
   - ❑ They're ashamed of what they did.
   - ❑ They're afraid of what their friends will say.
   - ❑ They think others will see them as hypocrites.
   - ❑ They're afraid of punishment.
   - ❑ They don't want to be humiliated in public.
   - ❑ They're afraid they will get a police record.
   - ❑ They're afraid they will get a bad reputation.
   - ❑ They'll have to stop doing what they're doing.
   - ❑ They think it's more fun if no one knows about it.

3. Jesse was caught with drugs in his locker during a check at school. As part of his punishment, he'll face time in juvenile hall, a huge fine, and the wrath of his parents.

   What do you think the punishment should be?

   Why?

4. Check out **Proverbs 28:13, Isaiah 29:15,** and **1 John 1:8-9** and complete the following sentences.

   It's a bad idea to try to hide _____. It's futile anyhow because God always _____. Better to _____ their sins because then people will find _____.

5. Should people ever confess their wrongdoings to someone else? Why or why not?

   If yes, who should people confess to?

   If you wanted to confess your wrongdoing, who would you go to now?

COMING CLEAN [confessing our sins—Proverbs 28]

THIS WEEK

Teenagers—like most human beings—find it hard to confess when they've done wrong. Sins can stay to haunt us and make us feel guilty. That's one reason that the Bible urges confession. It's a healthy cleansing process—the beginning of mercy and forgiveness. There's no reality check like admitting our failures. This TalkSheet session will encourage your students to be honest about their spiritual failures. Your kids will be challenged to quickly admit their sins to God.

OPENER

You may want to use this illustration (or one like it) to start things off. Before your meeting, fill a backpack with some large rocks. On each rock, write a sin (either on the rock or a piece of tape on the rock)—examples include lying, cheating, stealing, swearing, etc. Zip up the backpack or bag. During your intro, ask for some volunteers to come up to the front of the room. Have them put the backpack on and describe how it feels to have the pack on. Make a master list of the words that they use. Then open up the backpack and pull out the stones. Show that each stone has something written on it—a sin that needs confessing. Point out that just like the backpack, unconfessed sin wears people down—it's a burden that they carry around. Use this activity to jumpstart your discussion on confessing sins, getting forgiveness, and letting God carry the load.

THE DISCUSSION, BY NUMBERS

1. Have your students talk about which is easier and more brave—to hide or to conceal wrongdoing. What does God think about confessing sins? How can this bring you closer to God?

2. Why do people tend to cover up wrongdoing? What are the most common rankings among your group members? What are the dangers of covering up sins?

3. How do your kids think Jesse should be punished? Is having drugs in his locker a sin? Or is it just against the law? You may want to talk about other situations like this such as drinking alcohol or driving over the speed limit. Are these things sins, in God's eyes? Why or why not? Check out Romans 13:1-5.

4. Explore the teaching of the Bible on confession of sin and the uselessness of concealment. Discuss the all-knowing power of God and his desire to forgive and have mercy.

5. Talk about when and if people should confess their sins to another person and even ask for forgiveness. Who would your kids go to and why? How many of them would go to God first? If your kids want to talk with someone, what qualities do they look for in a confidante?

THE CLOSE

To follow up from the intro, pull out the rocks from the backpack. Remind your group that God takes their sins, like the rocks, and thrown them into the deepest part of the sea—they're gone forever. God lovingly offers forgiveness and mercy to those who learn the habit of confessing. And he's waiting for your kids to bring their distresses, concerns, and wrongdoings to him. He knows about them anyway and he's willing to listen. Encourage your kids to ask God for forgiveness—and if they need someone else to talk with, to find an adult (let them know that you're available, too). God forgives and forgets. Period. What's holding your kids back today?

MORE

● You may want to talk more about how holding sin in can affect trust and respect in relationships. How can unconfessed sin hurt a friendship, a relationship with a boyfriend or girlfriend, or relationships with parents? What happens when someone is caught in a sin? What happens when someone hurts someone else and doesn't ask for forgiveness? Challenge your kids to get right with the people that they've hurt and to get the burden of that sin off their back.

● If your group has a high level of trust, you may want to ask your kids to share one sin or cover-up of a sin (or lie) that they wish they could erase and why. Or have them write their responses on a paper anonymously and have a youth leader read all the response aloud. Remind your kids of the TalkSheet ground rule about confidentiality and group trust. Discuss the choices that your kids face. How do specific choices about sin affect a person's life?

WORDS TO LIVE BY

1. What do you think is the **most common** opinion of the Bible by people outside of the church?
   - ❏ The Bible is a documentation of historical events thousands of years ago.
   - ❏ The Bible was written by a great prophet named Jesus.
   - ❏ The Bible is not the word of God.
   - ❏ The Bible has some good stuff in it, such as the Golden Rule.
   - ❏ The Bible is something religious people argue over.
   - ❏ The Bible is just a book of wacky rules and teachings.
   - ❏ Other—

2. What do you think? Pick one response to complete the sentence.
   When people read the Bible, they should—
   - ❏ believe and follow only what their heart tells them to
   - ❏ believe and follow only what their church or pastor tells them to
   - ❏ study carefully, then obey what is clearly taught
   - ❏ interpret it any way they want to
   - ❏ see its contents as suggestions rather than strict guidelines
   - ❏ enjoy it as literature

3. Many religions have their own holy books. Some groups have added to—or taken away from—what is found in the Bible. What would you say to someone if they insisted that they had a new and improved version of God's Word?

4. Check out these verses and write down a few words that describe the attributes of the Bible.
   Proverbs 30:5
   Luke 11:28
   2 Timothy 3:15-16
   Hebrews 4:12

5. How much time do you spend reading the Bible during a week? 10 minutes? An hour? 3 hours? How does this compare with the time you spend on other activities?

WORDS TO LIVE BY [the Bible—Proverbs 30]

THIS WEEK

The writers of Proverbs tells people that every word of God is flawless. Human wisdom can't even come close to the incredible illumination that comes from God's word. Are your kids bored with the Bible? Do they find it dull and inapplicable to their lives? Through this TalkSheet, your kids will discover that God provides people a refuge, a rule of instruction for living life, a love letter, and an instrument for touching the most private aspects of their lives—all packaged in pages of paper and ink.

OPENER

Bring in an instruction book for any device—from a computer, TV, microwave, radio, DVD player, or the like. Ask your group how many of them (or their parents) actually read instruction books. How many tend to avoid them or only read them when they are stuck? Talk about how people can mess up their purchases by failing to follow the instruction manuals. Compare this with the Bible—God's instruction manual for human beings. How do people mess up their lives by not following his word?

THE DISCUSSION, BY NUMBERS

1. Discuss the various viewpoints that people have of the Bible. How are these opinions formed? Point out that the Bible is one of the most frequently sold books in the U.S. every year. Do non-Christians study the Bible? How does being a Christian change a person's perspective on the Bible?

2. How did your kids respond to this question? Point out that everyone is different—some people enjoy reading the Bible more than others. Is it fair to assume that all Christians should use the Bible in the same way? Why or why not?

3. Point out that the Bible has survived innumerable attacks, alterations, and other abuses, and still powerfully testifies to a risen Christ. What are the dangers in altering or adding to the Bible? Check out Revelation 22:18-19 with your group to see what God thinks.

4. What attributes did your group list? You may want to make a list of their responses. Discuss what the Bible says about itself. How does this information relate to the previous questions?

5. How much time do your kids spend reading the Bible? What makes it difficult to spend a lot of time reading it? Do some Christians read more than others? Is a person who doesn't spend a lot of time reading the Bible a weak or poor Christian? Why or why not?

THE CLOSE

Point out that it's important to spend time reading about God and his word in the Bible. You may want to brainstorm and format at least one devotional plan that your kids could implement during the week. What realistic, tangible goal will they set for themselves? How much are they willing to commit to spending time with God? And can they come through on their commitment?

Brainstorm ways your kids can get into the Bible. Recommend student versions of Bibles including the New Student Bible or the NIV Student Bible (Zondervan, www.zondervan.com). Encourage them to find a version of the Bible that works for them. If a typical NIV is too hard for them to understand, have them find a version that is easier to read. You may also want to suggest some study tools or have them check out some student Web sites (such as www.christianteens.net or www.teens4god.com) where your kids can download devotions, find information, and learn more about how to grow in their faith.

MORE

- You may want to consider doing an in-group Bible study with your group, or part of your group. There are oodles of tangible Bible resources out there for high school youth groups including *Downloading the Bible* and the *Creative Bible Lessons* series. For more information on these resources, check out www.YouthSpecialties.com.
- There are quite a few stimulating, challenging Bible trivia games available. These are great ways to teach your kids while learning new stuff, too! Play one of these games with your kids or create a Bible trivia game with your group. Have them write their own questions based on the Bible. The game could be played at your next meeting or retreat. You can find helpful Bible trivia questions at www.Biblequizzes.com or www.bible-trivia.com.

A WOMAN'S PLACE

1. Which roles do you think women can fill? Put an **arrow** by the ones you think they **can fill** and **cross out** the ones you think they **can't fill**.

Chef	Police officer	Surgeon
Soldier	Counselor	Firefighter
Weightlifter	Webmaster	Governor
Politician	Dentist	Computer consultant
Bible teacher	President	Businessperson
Mechanic	Truck driver	Theologian
Professional athlete	Scientist	Farmer
Pastor	Stockbroker	Construction worker

2. Some roles of wives and husbands have shifted over the last few years. Who do you think should do the following most or all of the time—**W (wife), H (husband),** or **B (both)**?

___ Do the shopping ___ Do the laundry
___ Cook the meals ___ Initiate sex
___ Take care of the kids ___ Make most of the money
___ Clean the house ___ Buy gifts and flowers
___ Service the car ___ Do households repairs
___ Go to the kids' sports games ___ Oversee finances
___ Work full-time ___ Discipline the kids
___ Be the spiritual leader ___ Do the yard work

3. Read **Proverbs 31:10-31** and make a list of the attributes of a godly woman.

4. If you're a female, what does the description of the woman in Proverbs 31 mean to you?

If you're a male, what does the description of the woman in Proverbs 31 tell you about women?

A WOMAN'S PLACE [the role of women—Proverbs 31]

THIS WEEK

Proverbs 31 describes a woman who loved, supported, and cared for her husband and children while
she actively participated in business and management. Her actions earned her the praise and respect
of all. The roles of men and women in different soci-
eties have shifted and changed over the years. This
may leave your kids confused about the value and
role of women today. This TalkSheet discusses what
God thinks about women and their abilities.

OPENER

How are women portrayed in society today? You
may want to bring in some magazine articles,
advertisements, or clips of TV shows or movies.
Show these to your kids and ask them how the
woman is being portrayed in this piece. Is the role
of the woman positive or negative? Why? What
assumptions about women could a person make,
based on these pieces of information? Spend some
time brainstorming how society and the media has
defined the role and worth of a woman. Make a list
of the positives and negatives that your kids think
of. Are women seen as successful and independent? Or are they degraded as sexual objects? How
are these roles different in the U.S. than in other
countries? Finally, how are the roles of women
today different than they were for their parents or
their grandparents?

THE DISCUSSION, BY NUMBERS

1. Talk about the roles that women have in our
   culture. Why are some roles unsuitable or inappro-
   priate for the typical woman? Are role restrictions
   based on common sense or on cultural traditions?
   What strengths or weaknesses do women have
   that would make certain roles better for them?

2. Your kids may have a variety of opinions on these
   items! Some may have strong opinions, based on
   how they grew up or what happens in their home.
   Talk about the roles that seemed designed for
   women and why women are better at some roles
   than men. Point out that marriage is a partnership—the husband and wife are a team. How do
   these roles change when a couple gets divorced?

3. Make a list of the attributes of women described
   in these verses. How would these roles be interpreted today?

4. Ask both the guys and girls to give feedback on
   what this proverb means to them. How did the
   results compare? Has the passage made them
   think differently about women? Why or why not?

THE CLOSE

God doesn't limit people because of their gender—
but he did create each person with different
strengths and weaknesses. Point out the balance
and industry that this woman had in her life and the
respect and love given to her by her husband and
family! The Bible emphasizes a balanced, healthy,
and servant-oriented outlook on gender roles (and
relationships in general!). How does this affect a
person's dating relationship or friendships with the
opposite sex? Based on these verses, how does God
want a man to treat a woman and vice versa?

MORE

● You may want to ask each student to write or suggest the characteristics they consider most important for an ideal mate. Record their opinions on a
  whiteboard or poster board. What different characteristics do your guys and girls look for? Why does
  each gender look for different characteristics?
  Does this vary by person? From the list they've
  made, what are the top three most important characteristics for a solid, healthy relationship?

● What damages a marriage or relationship? You
  may want to talk about the problems that couples
  face today. What challenges do they face in their
  roles? For example, how is a family affected if
  both parents work full time? Or if there's an
  abused partner or child in the family? How does
  divorce affect a family? Be sensitive to your group
  during this discussion. Many of them may be from
  broken homes or are dealing with problems at
  home. Has the change in women's roles weakened families today? Why or why not?

RESOURCES FROM YOUTH SPECIALTIES

YOUTH MINISTRY PROGRAMMING

Camps, Retreats, Missions, & Service Ideas (Ideas Library)
Compassionate Kids: Practical Ways to Involve Your Students in Mission and Service
Creative Bible Lessons from the Old Testament
Creative Bible Lessons in 1 & 2 Corinthians
Creative Bible Lessons in John: Encounters with Jesus
Creative Bible Lessons in Romans: Faith on Fire!
Creative Bible Lessons on the Life of Christ
Creative Bible Lessons in Psalms
Creative Junior High Programs from A to Z, Vol. 1 (A-M)
Creative Junior High Programs from A to Z, Vol. 2 (N-Z)
Creative Meetings, Bible Lessons, & Worship Ideas (Ideas Library)
Crowd Breakers & Mixers (Ideas Library)
Downloading the Bible Leader's Guide
Drama, Skits, & Sketches (Ideas Library)
Drama, Skits, & Sketches 2 (Ideas Library)
Dramatic Pauses
Everyday Object Lessons
Games (Ideas Library)
Games 2 (Ideas Library)
Games 3 (Ideas Library)
Good Sex: A Whole-Person Approach to Teenage Sexuality and God
Great Fundraising Ideas for Youth Groups
More Great Fundraising Ideas for Youth Groups
Great Retreats for Youth Groups
Holiday Ideas (Ideas Library)
Hot Illustrations for Youth Talks
More Hot Illustrations for Youth Talks
Still More Hot Illustrations for Youth Talks
Ideas Library on CD-ROM
Incredible Questionnaires for Youth Ministry
Junior High Game Nights
More Junior High Game Nights
Kickstarters: 101 Ingenious Intros to Just about Any Bible Lesson
Live the Life! Student Evangelism Training Kit
Memory Makers
The Next Level Leader's Guide
Play It! Over 150 Great Games for Youth Groups
Roaring Lambs
Special Events (Ideas Library)
Spontaneous Melodramas
Spontaneous Melodramas 2
Student Leadership Training Manual
Student Underground: An Event Curriculum on the Persecuted Church
Super Sketches for Youth Ministry
Talking the Walk
Teaching the Bible Creatively
Videos That Teach
What Would Jesus Do? Youth Leader's Kit
Wild Truth Bible Lessons
Wild Truth Bible Lessons 2
Wild Truth Bible Lessons—Pictures of God
Wild Truth Bible Lessons—Pictures of God 2
Worship Services for Youth Groups

PROFESSIONAL RESOURCES

Administration, Publicity, & Fundraising (Ideas Library)
Dynamic Communicators Workshop
Equipped to Serve: Volunteer Youth Worker Training Course
Help! I'm a Junior High Youth Worker!
Help! I'm a Small-Group Leader!
Help! I'm a Sunday School Teacher!
Help! I'm a Volunteer Youth Worker!
How to Expand Your Youth Ministry
How to Speak to Youth...and Keep Them Awake at the Same Time
Junior High Ministry (Updated & Expanded)
The Ministry of Nurture: A Youth Worker's Guide to Discipling Teenagers
Postmodern Youth Ministry
Purpose-Driven® Youth Ministry
Purpose-Driven® Youth Ministry Training Kit
So That's Why I Keep Doing This! 52 Devotional Stories for Youth Workers
A Youth Ministry Crash Course
Youth Ministry Management Tools
The Youth Worker's Handbook to Family Ministry

ACADEMIC RESOURCES

Four Views of Youth Ministry & the Church
Starting Right: Thinking Theologically About Youth Ministry

DISCUSSION STARTERS

Discussion & Lesson Starters (Ideas Library)
Discussion & Lesson Starters 2 (Ideas Library)
EdgeTV
Get 'Em Talking
Keep 'Em Talking!
Good Sex: A Whole-Person Approach to Teenage Sexuality & God
High School TalkSheets—Updated!
More High School TalkSheets—Updated!
High School TalkSheets Psalms and Proverbs—Updated!
Junior High and Middle School TalkSheets—Updated!
More Junior High and Middle School TalkSheets—Updated!
Junior High and Middle School TalkSheets Psalms and Proverbs—Updated!
Real Kids: Short Cuts
Real Kids: The Real Deal—on Friendship, Loneliness, Racism, & Suicide
Real Kids: The Real Deal—on Sexual Choices, Family Matters, & Loss
Real Kids: The Real Deal—on Stressing Out, Addictive Behavior, Great Comebacks, & Violence
Real Kids: Word on the Street
Unfinished Sentences: 450 Tantalizing Statement-Starters to Get Teenagers Talking & Thinking
What If...? 450 Thought-Provoking Questions to Get Teenagers Talking, Laughing, and Thinking
Would You Rather...? 465 Provocative Questions to Get Teenagers Talking
Have You Ever...? 450 Intriguing Questions Guaranteed to Get Teenagers Talking

ART SOURCE CLIP ART

Stark Raving Clip Art (print)
Youth Group Activities (print)
Clip Art Library Version 2.0 CD-ROM

DIGITAL RESOURCES

Clip Art Library Version 2.0 CD-RPOM
Ideas Library on CD-ROM
Youth Ministry Management Tools

VIDEOS AND VIDEO CURRICULUMS

Dynamic Communicators Workshop
EdgeTV
Equipped to Serve: Volunteer Youth Worker Training Course
The Heart of Youth Ministry: A Morning with Mike Yaconelli
Live the Life! Student Evangelism Training Kit
Purpose-Driven® Youth Ministry Training Kit
Real Kids: Short Cuts
Real Kids: The Real Deal—on Friendship, Loneliness, Racism, & Suicide
Real Kids: The Real Deal—on Sexual Choices, Family Matters, & Loss
Real Kids: The Real Deal—on Stressing Out, Addictive Behavior, Great Comebacks, & Violence
Real Kids: Word on the Street
Student Underground: An Event Curriculum on the Persecuted Church
Understanding Your Teenager Video Curriculum
Youth Ministry Outside the Lines: The Dangerous Wonder of Working with Teenagers

STUDENT RESOURCES

Downloading the Bible: A Rough Guide to the New Testament
Downloading the Bible: A Rough Guide to the Old Testament
Grow For It Journal through the Scriptures
So What Am I Gonna Do With My Life? Journaling Workbook for Students
Spiritual Challenge Journal: The Next Level
Teen Devotional Bible
What (Almost) Nobody Will Tell You about Sex
What Would Jesus Do? Spiritual Challenge Journal
Wild Truth Journal for Junior Highers
Wild Truth Journal—Pictures of God
Wild Truth Journal—Pictures of God 2